TASTING
OHIO

Favorite Recipes from
the Buckeye State

by **Sara Bir**

photography by Melanie Tienter
foreword by Bryn Mooth

FARCOUNTRY
PRESS

❧ For Scooter, Squiggy, and Smokey ❧

ISBN: 978-1-56037-690-3

© 2018 by Farcountry Press
Text © 2018 by Sara Bir
Photography © 2018 by Melanie Tienter
Back cover: Combing Brush Road, photo by Mike Tewkesbury
Pages ii: Windsor Covered Bridge, photo by Kenneth Keifer, Shutterstock

For more information about our books, write Farcountry Press, P.O. Box 5630,
Helena, MT 59604; call (800) 821-3874; or visit www.farcountrypress.com.

Library of Congress Cataloging-in-Publication Data

Names: Bir, Sara, 1976– author. | Tienter, Melanie, photographer.
Title: Tasting Ohio : favorite recipes from the Buckeye State / by Sara Bir ;
  photography by Melanie Tienter ; foreword by Bryn Mooth.
Description: Helena, MT : Farcountry Press, [2017] | Includes index.
Identifiers: LCCN 2017047651 | ISBN 9781560376903 (hardcover : alk. paper)
Subjects: LCSH: Cooking, American—Midwestern style. | Cooking—Ohio. |
  LCGFT: Cookbooks.
Classification: LCC TX715.2.M53 B565 2017 | DDC 641.59771—dc23
LC record available at https://lccn.loc.gov/2017047651

Produced in the United States of America. Printed in China.

22 21 20 19 18   1 2 3 4 5

contents

chapter 1: Breakfast & Brunch

chapter 2: Appetizers & Snacks

chapter 3: Salads & Sides

chapter 4: Soups & Stews

chapter 5: Main Courses

chapter 6: Desserts & Sweet Treats

acknowledgments

by Sara Bir

A cookbook, no matter how large or small, is a product of collaboration. The experience of compiling and testing the recipes for *Tasting Ohio* has connected—and reconnected—me with kind, talented, and generous people I am glad to have in my professional and personal life.

Photographer Melanie Tienter spent many hours fiddling with lighting and camera settings to get just the right shot. Her vision and humor transformed many a plate of food into something magical. This book is as much her work as it is mine.

Phoebe Thompson and Laurel Randolph stepped in as editorial assistants, each bringing a surge of positive energy and forward momentum.

Will Harmon, this book's editor, has consistently been encouraging, patient, understanding, and swift to respond to my smallest queries.

Tasting Kentucky author Maggie Green introduced me to this series and Farcountry Press, and I am thankful for the wisdom she readily shared about this type of cookbook. Carrie Havranek, my IACP BFF, is on her own cookbook journey with *Tasting Pennsylvania*, and having a trusted friend going through exactly what I was going through was motivating and comforting.

A childhood obsession with my mother's library of cookbooks planted the seeds of what is now my career. Her unwavering support and inspiration over the years has been instrumental in all aspects of my life. My parents, Jim and Carol Bir, have been my lifelong advocates and most enthusiastic eaters. I love you.

Caroline Waller lent us a key to her peaceful and stylish work space, Passiflora Studio, for a few heavenly photo shoots.

Nikki Butler often swooped in with excellent advice or a thoughtful pick-me-up at just the right moment. Just knowing she's my friend makes me smile.

Thanks and love to my husband and daughter who well know the sting of warnings not to eat some treat because it's for a recipe thing I'm working on.

Finally, I'd like to extend my gratitude to the chefs, business owners, and support staff who shared the recipes that make up this book. Daily working life for chefs carries many urgent demands. To have such talented people give their time and creative secrets to me is a gift I value tremendously. Their work is part of what makes Ohio such a rewarding place to live, work, grow, cook, and eat.

foreword

by Bryn Mooth

What is Ohio food? This would be an easier question to answer if there were one Ohio.

On the face of it, Ohio's three largest cities seem as distantly related as fourth cousins; they may share great-grandmama's DNA but have little else in common. Cleveland segues into the industrial Northeast; Columbus is solidly Midwestern with a kaleidoscopic pattern overlaid by the diverse student body of a major university; and Cincinnati dips its toes into western Appalachia and the South.

But these cities are linked by an immigrant past that reaches back to Germany and Eastern Europe, with a shared heritage of rib-sticking food and a certain frugality in the kitchen. (What's old is new: in today's foodie lingo, these old ways translate as comfort food and zero-waste cooking.) From Lake Erie to the Ohio River, Ohio food is—and always will be— goetta and city chicken and pierogi and cabbage rolls. And beer and the chicken dance. It's Sokolowski's University Inn in Cleveland, Schmidt's Sausage Haus in Columbus, and Mecklenburg Gardens in Cincinnati.

Today, Ohio food is putting a fresh spin on those traditional German and Polish favorites. Across the state, young chefs are reviving old methods like curing pork and fermenting sauerkraut, creating dishes that echo what our great-grandparents ate but still feel entirely contemporary.

And it's taking on global flavors beyond those of Eastern Europe. Chefs, food entrepreneurs, and home cooks who come to our state from around the world are still shaping Ohio food; it's just happening in a more micro-ethnic way—not just Asian and Latin American, but, for example, specifically Vietnamese and Argentinian. In a three-block radius in my adopted hometown of Cincinnati, I can get a chicken- and cheese-filled arepa made by Isis Arrieta-Dennis, who grew up in Colombia; a samosa prepared by a native of Nepal according to her family recipe; and a bowl of Japanese ramen with a side of Filipino chicharon.

Of course, Ohio food isn't exclusively international—much of what we eat, whether we're cooking at home or eating out, is intensely local,

informed by what our state's farmers grow and raise. It always has been. Ohio has a strong manufacturing sector, but it's also very agricultural— a leading producer of food products like wheat and beef and eggs. Ohio food was farm-to-table before farm-to-table became trendy. Ohio farmers Bob and Lee Jones bear no small responsibility for bringing the movement from its California roots to the Midwest. Started thirty-some years ago, the Chef's Garden, the family's pioneering farm in Milan (roughly halfway between Toledo and Cleveland) grows more than 2,000 varieties for top restaurants in the state and across the country, and their Culinary Vegetable Institute hosts chefs and visitors for work sessions and seminars that deepen the connection between the people who grow our food and the people who cook and eat it.

I've come to experience Ohio food as a native Hoosier who's now lived in Cincinnati for twenty-five years. To me, Ohio food encompasses the local produce, meats, and artisan bread I buy every week at Findlay Market, which has become sort of a spiritual home for my husband and me. It's roadside barbecue at Just Q'in in blink-and-miss-it Newtown; it's a burger at my beloved neighborhood tavern, Zip's; it's a bowl of soul-satisfying pasta Bolognese at Nicola's in Over-the-Rhine.

Global and local, traditional and contemporary: in *Tasting Ohio: Favorite Recipes from the Buckeye State*, Sara Bir manages to capture Ohio food in all its glorious forms. She's mapped out a culinary road trip we can experience from the comfort of our own kitchens, and since I love cooking at home, I'm eager to work my way through all of the recipes. (Although I'll confess that it's super tempting to hop in the car, bypass interstate seventy-what-ever in favor of two-lane state roads, and sample these dishes prepared by the folks who know them best.)

What is Ohio food? It's hard to put your finger on it, exactly. But I've discovered—and as Sara so graciously shares with you in these pages— that it's inviting, it's heartfelt, and, most of all, it's delicious.

introduction

People often describe Ohio by what it is not. I used to describe Ohio by what it is not. It is not on the coast of an ocean. It is not mountainous. It is not a world traveler's default destination with an iconic national park. It is not quite Appalachian, Midwestern, or Rust Belt, and yet it is miraculously all of those things.

Ohio is a place where American idylls bleed together to form one landmass shaped like a heart, glorious in its symmetry—if not geometric, then symmetrical in essence. Even its name is bookended with Os, as the oft-repeated riddle ("what's round on the ends and HI in the middle?") goes. Each chamber of that heart has a major city, many smaller cities, towns with unusual names, and folksy festivals devoted to pumpkins or sauerkraut or Ohio-grown grapes. Its northern and southern borders are each defined by large bodies of water that were crucial in the development of our country in its younger days and that continue to be economically and culturally influential.

Smack-dab in the center of the heart is its capital and largest city, Columbus. Its southern zones are rilled with the foothills of the Appalachians, and glacial grooves unlike any others in the country are carved in its northern extremes. Drive east toward Indiana and a flat expanse of prairie takes over. Across the state, the topography is still dotted with earthworks built by prehistoric indigenous tribes. We literally walk among the past.

When Ohio was first settled, it was as a gateway to western North America, what came to be known as the Northwest Territory. Veterans—mostly officers who'd served in the Revolutionary War—formed The Ohio Company and went to scout out plots of land to develop as potential communities. In 1788, they arrived in Marietta, the town where I grew up and now live. Settlers made quick work of clearing fields, building stately homes, and creating new towns. They gave the prehistoric earthworks Latin names. You could say they were Ohio's first immigrants.

In following decades, subsequent waves of immigrants came to Ohio too, giving its largest cities and most remote hollers their culinary personalities. Some came from other states; some came from other countries.

Newcomers continue to arrive in Ohio, continuing this fertile and dynamic cultural exchange of ingredients and flavor profiles.

There are many Ohios. Some are flat, some are hilly, some are rural, some are decidedly urban. Ask someone in Akron to name a regional dish, and they may say sauerkraut balls. A person from Columbus may say fried bologna sandwiches, and someone living in Portsmouth, along the Ohio River, might say chicken and noodles. That person in Portsmouth may speak with an undeniable twang, a vocal inflection that completely disappears among residents a mere two-hour drive north.

Ohio is home to so many small colleges and universities that I gave up trying to keep track of their names and locations long ago. It is also the home of eight presidents of the United States. The state tree, the Ohio buckeye, produces an inedible nut (you're much better off with the *trompe l'oeil* chocolate and peanut butter version). The state drink is tomato juice, a nod to Reynoldsburg resident Alexander Livingston, whose developments in the early 1900s modernized the tomato. The state's agricultural diversity is remarkable and important—agriculture is Ohio's largest industry, generating billions in revenue every year, from the biggest conventional farms to the smallest family-run operations.

Cooks and gardeners, take note: people here love to grow things, and they do so not to prove anything except that it gives them pleasure. Ohioans hit the hundreds of farmers markets that pop up in communities large and small not to make the scene, but to buy quality, locally grown foods from people they know by name. We visit U-Pick farms to collect berries, and we sit on porches in the summertime to snap garden-fresh green beans. We fetishize the freshness of summer sweet corn. When I was a kid, my family would travel to visit friends down South and bring along a box of homegrown tomatoes. "Ohio tomatoes!" they'd rave, and I couldn't quite pinpoint the source of their excitement. Only once I sampled tomatoes out of state did I get it. While juicy and ripe, they still seemed wan. Are Ohio tomatoes really better, or is it simply a state of mind we attach to them?

Thank goodness Ohio is not synonymous with glamour because we

enjoy a far better thing: freedom. For those who live here, the proof is in the pudding. It's the sum of the flavor of the tomato itself and the sensation of eating one grown in Ohio soil while standing on Ohio soil. That freedom—the tomato state of mind—is what lured me back here to stay.

Whether you're here to stay, just passing through, or returning after a long absence, we're happy you are here. Hang out and be yourself. We may not all see this place the same way, but that's the point. In Ohio, we still all belong.

Driving across Ohio, an abundance of unusual names tickles the tongue: Wapakoneta, Pataskala, Ashtabula, Gnadenhutten. And there are cities named after locations abroad: Toledo, Athens, Cadiz, Lima, Parma, Versailles. On a road trip, they are merely exits on highways, places to stop and fill up a gas tank and order from a drive-through in the interest of making good time. But if you can, drive into the town and look deeper. Make your time well spent. Each place has its own character, its own peculiar layers of history. Every restaurant, bed and breakfast, or institution that shared recipes for this book has its own story to tell. Some of *Tasting Ohio*'s contributors are native Ohioans and some came from elsewhere, bringing their own background to weave into the ever-expanding tapestry of our food landscape. My hope is that the following recipes will pique not just your hunger, but your curiosity. Talk to the people around you, and they will remind you of the wonders, edible and otherwise, sitting right at your feet.

—SARA BIR

guidelines for recipes

Equipment

❧ Oven temperatures are listed in degrees Fahrenheit. Unless the recipe recommends the convection setting, use the conventional settings on your oven.

❧ Generally speaking, go by the visual indicators in the recipe ("cook until saucy and the beef is no longer pink") rather than strictly by time ("about 6 minutes"). Every range differs in the power and stability of its heat levels. Using an oven thermometer can be a great help, particularly with baking; oven thermostats often are off by 25 degrees or more.

❧ If the success of a recipe depends on using a specific size pan, it will say so in the recipe; don't make substitutions. If the pan size is adaptable, go ahead and try, but cooking or baking times may differ from those given in the recipe.

❧ When a recipe calls for pureeing, you may use either a food processor, blender, or immersion blender. The recipe will call for the preferred piece of equipment, but if you don't have it, don't let that stop you from making the recipe.

Ingredients

❧ If no specific type of salt is called for, the default salt is regular table salt. Many recipes in the book call for kosher salt, which differs in weight per volume from other types of salt. If you are swapping one variety of salt for another, be sure to taste as you go. (Actually, tasting as you go is always a good idea!)

❧ Unless specified, the all-purpose flour called for in recipes is unbleached all-purpose flour. To measure flour for recipes in this book, spoon the flour lightly into the correct size dry measuring cup and level with a metal spatula or table knife.

- The butter called for in these recipes is unsalted butter. Do not substitute margarine for butter.

- Unless stated otherwise, sugar refers to granulated white sugar. Brown sugar may be either light or dark, unless the recipe calls for one style.

- Many of these recipes call for heavy cream, occasionally quite a bit of it. If you've ever wondered why you love eating out, now you know! Generally speaking, if using the generous amount of cream called for in some of these recipes makes you uncomfortable, I'd recommend not making the recipe, because reducing the amount of cream or substituting another dairy product can yield vastly different results.

- Recipes that feature grated cheese give the amount by weight (in ounces) and then by volume (in cups). Grated cheeses vary in volume depending on their hardness and moisture content and whether they are coarsely or finely grated. Look for the weight when purchasing cheese and then portion it accordingly when making the dish. Fortunately, cheese is not an ingredient that demands precision—a little more or less won't significantly affect your results. It's best to buy cheese in block form; pre-grated cheese tends to quickly lose flavor, is more expensive, and often contains additives to prevent clumping.

- The heat level of both fresh and dry chiles, as well as ground chiles, can vary quite a bit. It's a good idea to taste a tiny bit of fresh chile peppers before adding the whole mess to a recipe. Likewise, the heat level of dry spices can decline with age. If the recipe gives a range, begin by adding a lesser amount and increase the level according to your preference.

- Recipes calling for broth or stock use low-sodium store-bought stock. If using homemade, you may need to adjust the seasoning accordingly.

- Several recipes feature roasted garlic. To roast garlic, preheat the oven to 400 degrees. Cut the tops off one or more heads of garlic and rub a little olive oil on the cut surfaces. Wrap the garlic loosely in foil and roast until golden brown and very soft, 40 to 60 minutes.

Breakfast & Brunch

Cinnamon Chip Scones, p. 8

Nonstick cooking spray

1 ¼ cups pecans or walnuts, toasted (see Note)

1 cup brown rice flour

¼ cup tapioca flour

½ teaspoon baking powder

¼ teaspoon baking soda

½ teaspoon ground cinnamon

½ teaspoon fine sea salt

1 cup lightly mashed ripe banana (2 to 3 bananas)

½ cup milk

⅓ cup vegetable oil

½ teaspoon vanilla extract

2 large eggs, separated

Turbinado sugar, for garnish (optional)

Makes 12 muffins

☙ *Note: To toast nuts, spread them on a rimmed baking sheet and toast in a preheated 350-degree oven until fragrant, about 5 minutes.*

Banana Nut Muffins

EASTER HOUSE BED & BREAKFAST, ADA
INNKEEPER AMY EDDINGS

Amy Eddings has an uncommon career combination: broadcaster and innkeeper. She was a National Public Radio host for WNYC for fifteen years. She and her husband, Mark, traded in city life and bought property in Ada, where they restored a Queen Anne Victorian house and opened the only bed and breakfast for miles around. Eddings (who's now with Cleveland's WCPN) loves these little muffins, which rely on toasted pecans and the bananas themselves for sweetness, rather than added sugar. They're gluten-free and especially tender.

Preheat the oven to 375 degrees with a rack in the center of the oven. Line a 12-cup muffin tin with paper liners and lightly spray the liners with cooking spray.

Very finely chop the cooled, toasted pecans with a knife or by pulsing in a food processor (don't go too far or the nuts will turn to paste). Set aside 3 tablespoons for garnishing.

In a large bowl, combine the remaining chopped pecans, brown rice flour, tapioca flour, baking powder, baking soda, cinnamon, and salt.

In a medium bowl, whisk together the bananas, milk, oil, vanilla, and egg yolks.

In the bowl of an electric mixer, whip the egg whites on medium-high speed until they form soft peaks. Fold the banana mixture into the nut-flour mixture until combined (don't worry about small lumps). Fold one-third of the whipped egg whites into the batter, then gently fold in the remaining egg whites until just combined (it's okay if some egg white streaks remain).

Fill each muffin tin about three-quarters full of batter (an ice cream scoop works well). Sprinkle with the reserved ground pecans and turbinado sugar (if using). Bake until the muffins are golden brown and rounded on top, 25 to 30 minutes. Set the tin on a wire rack and cool for 3 minutes, then remove the muffins from the tin and set on the rack to cool completely.

Gnocchi

1 large russet potato (11 to 12 ounces), whole and unpeeled

1 cup all-purpose flour, plus extra for dusting

½ teaspoon kosher salt

To assemble

4 ounces ground chorizo

2 tablespoons unsalted butter, divided

2 scallions, thinly sliced

2 eggs

Salt and freshly ground black pepper

2 ounces (½ cup) grated white Cheddar cheese

Serves 2

Breakfast Gnocchi

TOLEDO MUSEUM OF ART CAFÉ, TOLEDO   CHEF JOE FELIX

Renowned for its glass collection and community outreach programs, the Toledo Museum of Art is a can't-miss destination when in the Glass City. Admission is free, and the exhibitions are compelling and diverse. Make a stop at the museum's café, where Chef Felix serves handmade gnocchi in many menu items, including this fabulous breakfast gnocchi. Searing the gnocchi in a hot pan makes its texture exciting: chewy on the outside, fluffy on the inside.

For the gnocchi:
Place the potato in a pot and cover with cold salted water. Boil until the potato easily pierces with a fork, 30 to 45 minutes. Drain, cut into quarters, and run through a ricer or food mill while still warm. Discard the peels.

Line a rimmed baking sheet with a lightly floured kitchen towel.

In a medium bowl, mix the riced potato with the flour and kosher salt, kneading the dough just until it comes together and doesn't crack when pressed. Cut into quarters and roll each into a ½-inch-thick rope. Cut each rope into ½-inch pieces. Roll each piece across a wooden gnocchi board or the tines of a fork and drop onto the towel-lined baking sheet. Cover with plastic wrap or a slightly damp towel. (Gnocchi may be made up to 4 hours in advance and refrigerated.)

To assemble:
Crumble the chorizo in a medium skillet over medium heat. Cook, breaking up with a wooden spoon, until nicely browned and no pink spots remain. Drain off most but not all the grease. Reduce heat to low.

(continued on page 4)

Bring a large pot of salted water to a gentle boil. Add the gnocchi. When they have floated to the top for 30 seconds, drain, reserving about ¼ cup of the cooking water.

In another medium skillet, melt 1 tablespoon of the butter over medium-high heat. Add the drained gnocchi and cook until brown in spots, 3 to 5 minutes. Add half the scallions and cook for 30 seconds. Add the cooked chorizo, plus a tablespoon or two of the reserved gnocchi cooking water. Toss gently to combine.

Melt the remaining tablespoon butter in a nonstick or cast-iron skillet over medium-low heat and cook the eggs just until the whites are set and the yolks are a bit runny. Season with salt and pepper. Divide the gnocchi between two serving bowls, sprinkle with the cheese, top with the fried eggs, and scatter the remaining scallions on top. Serve immediately.

Brunch Potatoes

THE FEVE, OBERLIN ❧ CHEF JASON ADELMAN

The Feve (say Fehv) was voted best brunch in Ohio by Ohio Magazine *readers, and potatoes like this prove why. Aromatic with the evocative smells of herbs de Provence and plump roasted garlic cloves, they are no humble afterthought. Cooking them low and slow in a skillet ensures they get nice and crispy, compelling you to want seconds. Get these going before you make your other breakfast components, and by the time everything else is ready, the potatoes will be perfect.*

1 head garlic

8 medium Yukon Gold potatoes
  (about 2½ pounds),
  cut into 1-inch cubes

4 tablespoons unsalted butter

1 teaspoon herbs de Provence,
  or to taste

Kosher salt

Serves 6 to 8

Preheat the oven to 350 degrees. Break the head of garlic into individual skin-on cloves. Scatter on a small rimmed baking sheet and roast until the cloves are soft when squeezed, 20 to 40 minutes. Peel and set aside. (The garlic may be roasted up to 4 days in advance.)

Put the cubed potatoes in a medium saucepan. Add water to cover. Bring to a boil and generously salt the water. Reduce to a simmer and cook gently until the potatoes are soft but still keep their shape, 10 to 20 minutes. Drain.

Heat a 12-inch heavy-bottomed skillet (preferably cast iron) to medium heat. Melt the butter, add the drained potatoes, and toss to coat in the butter. Season with the herbs de Provence and salt. Cook, stirring every few minutes, until brown and crunchy on most sides, 20 to 30 minutes. Add the garlic cloves and continue cooking another 10 minutes. Taste and season with more salt, if needed. Either serve immediately or allow to sit for up to an hour over low heat, stirring occasionally (don't let the garlic sit too long or it will burn).

Cinnamon sugar

¼ cup sugar

1 tablespoon cinnamon

Cinnamon angels

1 croissant

Softened unsalted butter,
    for spreading

About ½ teaspoon cinnamon sugar

Serves 1

Cinnamon Angels

SYCAMORE FARMS COUNTRY INN, OXFORD
INNKEEPER CHERRYL FORTÉ

Deceptively simple, these buttery breakfast treats are a cinnamon toast upgrade. They're a great use for day-old croissants—so much so that you may buy croissants just to make them.

For the cinnamon sugar:
In a small bowl, stir together the sugar and cinnamon.

To make the cinnamon angels:
Preheat the broiler.

Slice the croissant lengthwise, almost all the way through. Place on an ungreased baking sheet and open up the two halves flat, like an angel with wings. Spread the butter thinly on the cut surfaces and sprinkle generously with the cinnamon sugar. Broil, watching carefully the entire time, until the sugar starts to bubble and the edges of the croissant brown, 1 to 3 minutes, depending on your broiler.

Serve immediately with a fruit course, or as an accent to a savory dish.

❧ **Note:** *You'll have more cinnamon sugar than you need, but it will stay fresh for up to 6 months in a covered glass jar.*

3¼ cups all-purpose flour

⅓ cup plus 2 tablespoons sugar, divided

2½ teaspoons baking powder

½ teaspoon baking soda

½ teaspoon salt

¾ cup (1½ sticks) unsalted butter, cold, cut into small chunks

1 cup buttermilk

1 (10-ounce) package cinnamon baking chips

2 tablespoons unsalted butter, melted

Makes 12 scones

Cinnamon Chip Scones

THE 1861 INN, BATAVIA INNKEEPER CAROLE COTTRILL

A surprise ingredient—aromatic cinnamon chips—adds a warming spice to these rich and tender scones. They are one of The 1861 Inn's most frequently requested recipes.

Preheat the oven to 425 degrees. Line two large baking sheets with parchment paper.

In a large bowl, whisk together the flour, ⅓ cup sugar, baking powder, baking soda, and salt. Add the cold butter and work it in with a pastry cutter until the mixture forms coarse crumbs and no pieces of butter larger than a pea remain. With a rubber spatula, stir in the buttermilk just until moistened—the dough should be shaggy and a little sticky, but not dry. Dribble in 1 to 2 tablespoons of additional buttermilk, if necessary. Work in the cinnamon chips.

Turn the dough onto a lightly floured surface and knead gently 5 to 6 times. Divide in half and gently form each half into a 7-inch circle. Brush with melted butter and sprinkle with the remaining 2 tablespoons sugar.

Cut each circle into six wedges. Arrange on the baking sheets and bake until lightly browned, 10 to 13 minutes. Serve warm. The scones are best enjoyed the day they are made, but leftovers can be warmed for 5 minutes in a 350-degree oven.

❧ **Note:** *Cinnamon baking chips can be hard to find in grocery stores. The most readily available brand is Hershey's, and they can be ordered online from King Arthur Flour.*

Poultry seasoning

2 teaspoons ground dried sage

1½ teaspoons dried thyme

1 teaspoon dried marjoram

¾ teaspoon ground dried rosemary

½ teaspoon nutmeg

Goetta

4 cups low-sodium beef stock

4 cups water

2½ cups steel-cut oats

2 pounds ground pork shoulder

2 cups minced onion
    (about 2 medium onions)

4 garlic cloves, minced

1 bay leaf

1 teaspoon poultry seasoning

¼ teaspoon cayenne pepper

1½ teaspoons freshly ground
    white pepper

2 teaspoons kosher salt

Makes two 8½ x 4½ x 2½-inch
loaf pans

Goetta

SARA BIR, THE SAUSAGETARIAN

The strong German influence on Cincinnati lives on in the popularity of goetta (pronounced GET-uh), a regional breakfast meat made of ground pork (and sometimes beef) bound with oats. Think of it as scrapple's cousin. It's sold in southwest Ohio in grocery stores and independent meat markets, but it's not difficult to make at home. The harder part? Griddling dense and mushy slices of cooked goetta so they're nice and crispy—similar to hash browns, the enjoyment of goetta is all about texture.

For the poultry seasoning:
Combine all the ingredients in a small bowl. Store in a small jar for up to 6 months.

For the goetta:
In a large, heavy-bottomed pot, bring the beef stock and water to a boil. Stir in the oats, lower the heat to medium, and return to a boil. Reduce to a simmer and crumble in the ground meat, stirring with a sturdy wooden spoon to create a sludgy paste. Add the onions, garlic, and seasonings.

Reduce the heat as low as it can go and cook for at least 4 hours, stirring often (the oats tend to stick to the bottom and scorch as the mixture thickens). Alternatively, you can transfer the mixture to a slow cooker and cook on medium for about 6 hours, stirring every 30 to 60 minutes.

The goetta is ready when it's thick enough that a spoon can stand up in it. It should require a lot of oomph to stir at this point and resemble very stiff oatmeal. (When in doubt, err on the side of cooking it 30 to 60 minutes longer.) Taste the goetta and adjust the seasoning, if needed—it should be highly seasoned. Remove the bay leaf.

(continued on page 10)

Line two 8½ x 4½ x 2½-inch loaf pans with foil and grease the foil. Divide the mixture between the pans and let cool, uncovered, on the counter for about an hour before transferring to the refrigerator, still uncovered (this helps the goetta firm up better). Let the goetta set for at least 12 hours before slicing.

To cook the goetta, cut it crosswise into slices about ½ inch thick. Heat 1 tablespoon vegetable oil or bacon grease in a skillet (preferably nonstick or cast iron) over medium heat. Add the goetta slices, being careful not to crowd the pan, and cook for 10 to 15 minutes per side, disturbing it as little as possible so you don't break up the crispy brown crust as it forms.

☙ *Note: If possible, grind your own pork. Goetta freezes very well. You can cut the loaf into smaller segments, wrap them well, and freeze for up to 1 year.*

Frittata

Butter, for greasing the pan

2 teaspoons olive oil

9 ounces goetta, sliced
½ inch thick

12 eggs, beaten

2 cups heavy cream

2 tablespoons sliced chives

Pinch dried rosemary

1 teaspoon kosher salt

⅛ teaspoon freshly ground
black pepper

1½ ounces (½ cup) shredded
Gruyère cheese

1½ ounces (½ cup) shredded
white Cheddar cheese

Mustard vinaigrette

3 tablespoons champagne
or rice wine vinegar

1 tablespoon honey

¼ cup chopped fresh basil

1½ teaspoons stone-ground mustard

2 tablespoons roughly
chopped shallot

½ cup extra-virgin olive oil

½ teaspoon kosher salt

¼ teaspoon freshly ground
white pepper

Goetta Frittata with Watercress and Apple Salad

SLEEPY BEE CAFÉ, CINCINNATI
EXECUTIVE CHEF FRANCES KRONER

Breakfast-lovers in the Cincinnati region have typically served goetta as a side with eggs and toast, but today's chefs have begun incorporating goetta into recipes more creatively. At the weekend brunch hotspot Sleepy Bee Café, Chef Kroner pairs this rich, custardy frittata with a tangy, crunchy salad. It's a great make-ahead dish for a brunch at your own home.

For the frittata:
Preheat the oven to 325 degrees with a rack in the center of the oven.

Butter a 10 x 2½–inch springform pan. Set the pan on a piece of foil about 20 inches long. Fold the foil around the pan's edges as a protective blanket to catch any custard that tries to escape during cooking.

Pour a light layer of olive oil into the bottom of a large skillet over medium heat. Once the oil is hot, lay the sliced goetta in the pan and cook until nicely browned and crispy at the edges, 5 to 10 minutes per side. Drain the cooked goetta on paper towels.

Combine the eggs, cream, chives, rosemary, salt, and pepper in a large bowl and whisk until fully incorporated. (Using an immersion blender works well, too.) With a rubber spatula, fold in the cheese and browned goetta. Scrape into the prepared pan and cover using the excess foil overhanging the pan, being careful not to drape it in the egg mixture.

(continued on page 12)

To serve

2 bunches of watercress or arugula

2 Granny Smith apples, cored
   and thinly sliced into
   half-moons

Serves 6 to 12

Bake for 40 minutes, then carefully peel back the foil top and check for doneness. When the center is a bit jiggly but the rest is set, remove the foil and return the frittata to the oven for an additional 5 to 15 minutes. Let rest for 10 minutes before slicing.

For the mustard vinaigrette:
Combine the vinegar, honey, basil, mustard, and shallots in the jar of a blender. Mix at low speed until smooth. Increase the blender speed to medium and slowly add the olive oil in a thin stream until creamy and emulsified. Dip a piece of watercress or arugula in the dressing to taste for seasoning, then adjust seasoning to taste with salt and white pepper.

To serve:
Toss the greens with about ¼ cup of the vinaigrette. Cut the frittata into wedges and serve with the dressed salad garnished with apple slices.

Nonstick cooking spray

6 large eggs

½ teaspoon dried oregano

½ teaspoon dried basil

½ teaspoon kosher salt

¼ teaspoon freshly ground
   black pepper

1 cup milk

1 tablespoon olive oil

1 garlic clove, peeled
   and cut in half

4 cups fresh baby spinach leaves

½ cup crumbled feta cheese

2 ounces (½ cup) grated Swiss,
   Muenster, or Cheddar cheese

3 Roma tomatoes,
   sliced ¼ inch thick

Serves 6 to 8

Greek Breakfast Strata

THE WHITE OAK INN, DANVILLE
YVONNE MARTIN, INNKEEPER

Yvonne and Ian Martin began a second career when they moved to Knox County's Amish country and opened a bed and breakfast, where they serve meals made with local eggs and produce from their garden. With a green salad on the side, this quiche-like strata would make a fine light lunch or dinner.

Preheat the oven to 350 degrees. Spray a deep 9-inch pie dish with nonstick cooking spray.

In a large bowl, beat the eggs, oregano, basil, salt, and pepper until combined. Stir in the milk.

Heat the olive oil in a large skillet over low heat. Add the garlic and cook for 1 minute. Remove and discard the garlic. Increase the heat to medium, add the spinach to the skillet, and cook until just wilted. Transfer the spinach to the pie dish.

Sprinkle both cheeses over the spinach. Pour the egg mixture over the cheeses. Arrange the tomato slices on top. Bake until a knife inserted in the center comes out clean, 45 to 60 minutes. Let the strata stand for 10 minutes before cutting and serving.

4 cups old-fashioned rolled oats

½ cup shredded coconut

½ cup wheat germ

1 ½ teaspoons cinnamon

½ teaspoon ground nutmeg

½ cup vegetable oil

½ cup honey

¾ cup raisins (dark or light)

Makes about 7 cups

Homemade Granola

THE INN & SPA AT CEDAR FALLS, LOGAN
CHEF ANTHONY SCHULZ

This is a classic granola recipe, timelessly appealing with a cozy touch of warming spices. Guests at The Inn & Spa at Cedar Falls can fuel up on a wholesome bowl before setting out to explore the lush Hocking Hills.

Preheat the oven to 350 degrees.

Mix the oats, coconut, wheat germ, cinnamon, and nutmeg in a large bowl. Add the oil and honey and mix thoroughly with a sturdy wooden spoon.

Spread the mixture on an ungreased rimmed baking sheet and bake for 18 minutes, stirring every 6 minutes. Remove from the oven and put back into the large bowl. Mix in the raisins and allow to cool (granola will crisp up as it cools). Store in an airtight container for up to 1 month.

Streusel

⅓ cup all-purpose flour

⅓ cup sugar

1½ tablespoons unsalted butter, softened

Glaze

2 tablespoons sugar

1½ tablespoons freshly squeezed lemon juice

Batter

1½ cups pastry flour or all-purpose flour

1 cup sugar

¼ teaspoon baking soda

¼ teaspoon salt

2 large eggs

½ cup sour cream

½ cup (1 stick) unsalted butter, melted

1½ teaspoons freshly squeezed lemon juice

1 tablespoon grated lemon rind

Makes 12 muffins

Lemon Crumb Muffins

THE GRANARY AT PINE TREE BARN, WOOSTER

These sunny-tasting muffins are tender, cakey, and particularly moist from a lemon and sugar glaze poured over them right after they come out of the oven. They make a wonderful snack with tea or coffee, and they're quite easy to make. For years they've been a customer favorite at The Granary, the restaurant on the grounds of Pine Tree Barn, a family-run Christmas tree farm and furniture studio.

For the streusel:
In a medium bowl, whisk together the flour and sugar. Add the softened butter, working with your fingers until well incorporated but crumbly.

For the glaze:
Combine the sugar and lemon juice in a small bowl and stir until the sugar dissolves. Set aside.

For the batter:
Preheat the oven to 350 degrees. Grease a standard–size 12–muffin tin well.

Sift together the flour, sugar, baking soda, and salt in a medium bowl. Set aside.

Whisk the eggs in a large bowl. Beat in the sour cream, butter, and lemon juice until smooth. Fold in the lemon rind, then the flour mixture until well blended. The batter will be a little thick. Fill each muffin cup with about ¼ cup batter and top with about 1 tablespoon of the streusel. Bake until a toothpick inserted in the center comes out free of crumbs, 18 to 20 minutes.

Set the muffin tin on a wire rack. Poke the top of each muffin 15 to 20 times with a toothpick, then drizzle the tops with the glaze. Remove the muffins from the tin and cool. Serve warm or at room temperature. Store in an airtight container for up to 3 days.

❧ **Note:** *The Granary uses Softex pastry flour for its muffins. Pastry flour can be hard to find; muffins made with all-purpose flour won't be quite as light, but they will still be delicious and totally worth making.*

Caramel sauce

1 cup brown sugar (light or dark)

1 cup heavy cream

4 tablespoons unsalted butter

1 teaspoon vanilla extract
    or bourbon

Pinch salt

Pancakes

2¼ cups buttermilk

2 cups rolled oats (not instant)

¼ cup Greek yogurt
    (plain or vanilla)

1 teaspoon vanilla extract

½ cup oat flour or all-purpose flour

2 tablespoons granulated sugar

1 teaspoon salt

1 teaspoon baking soda

1 teaspoon baking powder

1 teaspoon cinnamon

4 tablespoons unsalted butter

2 eggs, beaten

To serve

2 peaches or nectarines,
    pitted and cut into matchsticks

Serves 4 to 6

Oat Pancakes with Caramel Sauce ("Happiness on a Plate")

BRICK HOUSE ON MAIN BED AND BREAKFAST, GNADENHUTTEN
INNKEEPER CATHY MARKER

Fluffy and nutty tasting, these pancakes stick to your ribs without weighing you down. The rolled oats in the batter have an overnight soak in butter-milk to soften them up, so plan to start the night before you want to serve these. To really go over the top, serve these pancakes with fresh peaches or nectarines and homemade caramel sauce.

For the caramel sauce:

Combine the brown sugar and cream in a medium heavy-bottomed saucepan. Cook over medium heat, stirring, until the sugar dissolves. Increase the heat to medium-high, bring to a full rolling boil, and cook for 2 minutes. Add the butter and gently swirl the pan to blend. Once the butter is incorporated, return to a boil and cook for 1 minute. Remove from heat and add the vanilla or bourbon and salt. Swirl to blend. Keep the sauce warm until the pancakes are ready to serve. If it seems too thick, you can add 1 to 2 tablespoons of cream before serving, swirling the pan to blend. Leftover sauce will keep, covered and refrigerated, for 2 weeks. Rewarm before using.

For the pancakes:

The night before serving, combine the buttermilk, oats, yogurt, and vanilla extract in a large bowl. Stir well, cover, and set in a cool place overnight. Sift together the flour, sugar, salt, baking soda, baking powder, and cinnamon in a small bowl. Set aside until morning.

(continued on page 18)

The following morning, melt the butter, cool slightly, and stir into the oats. Then add the eggs and beat until combined. Add the flour mixture to the oat mixture and stir just until mixed. Allow to stand at least 10 to 20 minutes before cooking.

Heat a nonstick electric griddle to 325 degrees. Pour ¼ to ½ cup batter on the griddle and cook until the edges are set and bubbles appear in the center of the pancake, about 2 minutes. Flip and cook until golden brown, about 2 more minutes. Serve at once or keep warm in a 180–degree oven for up to 30 minutes. Leftover batter can be covered and refrigerated to cook the next day.

To serve:
Plate the pancakes, pile the peach or nectarine matchsticks on top, and drizzle with the caramel sauce.

❧ **Note:** *This recipe is gluten-free if you use oat flour instead of all-purpose flour.*

Dough

¾ cup fine almond flour

⅓ cup sugar

1 scant tablespoon active dry yeast (one ¼-ounce packet)

1 teaspoon kosher salt

½ teaspoon ground cardamom

3 to 4 cups all-purpose flour

1 egg, beaten

¾ cup buttermilk

½ cup tepid water

2 teaspoons vanilla extract

6 tablespoons unsalted butter, softened

Brown sugar maple topping

1 cup brown sugar

¼ cup maple syrup

2 tablespoons water

½ cup (1 stick) unsalted butter

½ teaspoon vanilla extract

Orange raisin filling

¾ cup golden raisins

Juice of 1 orange

2 tablespoons orange liqueur, such as Grand Marnier or Triple Sec (optional)

¼ cup granulated sugar

¼ cup brown sugar

Orange and Pecan Cinnamon Sticky Buns with Orange Cream Cheese Icing

ARTHUR MORGAN HOUSE, YELLOW SPRINGS
CHEF ERIN CAMPBELL

You'll need a fork to best enjoy these pleasantly gooey buns. For a special-occasion brunch, let the shaped rolls rise overnight and pop them in the oven the following morning.

For the dough:
In the bowl of a stand mixer, whisk together the almond flour, sugar, yeast, salt, cardamom, and 3 cups of the all-purpose flour. Add the egg, buttermilk, water, and vanilla and mix on medium-low speed with a dough hook until the dough comes together. If the dough is too loose, add up to 1 cup more flour (dough should be a little sticky). As the mixer runs, add the butter in chunks and continue mixing until the dough is smooth and pulls away from the sides of the bowl, about 10 minutes.

Place in a large buttered mixing bowl, turn to coat, and cover with plastic wrap. Let rise until doubled in bulk, about 2 hours. Meanwhile, make the topping, filling, and icing.

For the brown sugar maple topping:
In a medium saucepan over medium-low heat, whisk together all the ingredients until the butter is melted and the sugar is dissolved. Divide the mixture evenly into two 8 x 8-inch baking pans and set aside.

(continued on page 20)

1 teaspoon cinnamon

Pinch ground cloves

Finely grated zest of 1 orange

¾ cup chopped toasted pecans, divided

4 tablespoons unsalted butter, melted

Orange cream cheese icing

8 ounces cream cheese, softened

1 tablespoon maple syrup

2 tablespoons freshly squeezed orange juice

2 teaspoons orange zest

1 teaspoon vanilla extract

3 to 6 tablespoons powdered sugar

Makes 12 rolls

For the orange raisin filling:
Combine the raisins, orange juice, and liqueur (if using) in a small saucepan. Simmer over medium-low heat until the liquid is just barely evaporated. Cover and set aside to steep.

In a small bowl, use your fingers to mix the sugars, spices, orange zest, and ½ cup of the pecans. Set aside.

For the orange cream cheese icing:
In a medium bowl, beat the cream cheese until smooth. Add the maple syrup, orange juice and zest, vanilla, and 3 tablespoons of the powdered sugar. If the icing is too loose, add more powdered sugar, 1 tablespoon at a time. Set aside.

To shape, bake, and ice the rolls:
Brush the sides of the pans with melted butter. Turn the dough onto a lightly floured countertop. Using your hands, gently press into an 18 x 9-inch rectangle, with the long edge facing you. Brush with the remaining melted butter, then sprinkle with the raisins and pecan-sugar mixture.

Carefully roll up the dough toward you and pinch the seam shut. Keeping the roll seam side down, slice into twelve equal pieces. Put six slices cut side up in each of the baking pans containing the brown sugar maple topping. Sprinkle with the reserved pecans. Cover the pans with plastic wrap. You may either let the rolls rise overnight in the refrigerator or let them rise on the counter until nearly doubled and touching each other, about 30 minutes.

Preheat the oven to 350 degrees. If baking the rolls after refrigerating overnight, let them stand at room temperature as the oven heats. Set the pans on sheets of foil to catch any topping that may bubble over. Bake until golden brown and bubbly, 25 to 35 minutes. Let the pans cool for a few minutes, then loosen the sides with a thin metal spatula and invert onto platters. Cool slightly, top with the icing, and serve.

❧ *Note: You may omit the almond flour and substitute another ½ cup all-purpose flour. To toast the nuts, spread them on a rimmed baking sheet and cook in a preheated 350-degree oven until fragrant, about 5 minutes.*

1 cup pawpaw pulp

1 cup whole milk buttermilk

¼ to ⅓ cup cold water

2 to 3 teaspoons sugar

Ground mace, nutmeg,
    or cumin for sprinkling

Serves 2 to 4

Pawpaw Lassi

SARA BIR, THE SAUSAGETARIAN

Pawpaw trees are native to North America and can be found growing wild in forests all over Ohio. The fruit of the pawpaw tree is not only edible but distinctively delicious, with a tropical flair and a custardy texture. Attendance at the Ohio Pawpaw Festival in Albany grows every year, and Ohio's craft brewers have led the way in brewing fruit beers with pawpaw.

A creamy and refreshing lassi is a wonderful way to enjoy pawpaws. You can enjoy this in lieu of a breakfast smoothie, or have a small glass as a snack. For the best texture and flavor, use full-fat buttermilk.

Combine the pawpaw pulp, buttermilk, water, and 2 teaspoons of the sugar in a bowl or large glass measuring cup and whisk until combined. If you want a smoother texture, use a blender.

Taste and add more sugar, if needed. You're aiming for this to be very balanced: sweet, tart, creamy, fruity. If it's too thick to be pourable, thin it out with a few tablespoons of water at a time.

Divide between glasses and garnish with a sprinkle of mace, nutmeg, or—for a savory hint—cumin. Serve immediately. Store leftovers covered in the refrigerator for up to a day.

❧ **Note:** *Pawpaws are very delicate and do not travel well, so they are not sold in grocery stores. During pawpaw season (mid-September to early October) you may find a vendor selling them at a farmers market, or you can forage for your own.*

Raspberry butter

2 cups (4 sticks) unsalted butter, at room temperature

1 cup fresh or frozen ripe raspberries, rinsed (thawed if frozen)

Raspberry sour cream coffee cake

Baking spray

2 cups all-purpose flour

1 tablespoon baking powder

¼ teaspoon salt

¾ cup dark brown sugar

2 cups pecans, chopped

1 tablespoon cinnamon

1 cup raspberry butter, softened

2 cups granulated sugar

2 eggs

2 cups sour cream

1 cup fresh raspberries

Powdered sugar, for garnish

Serves 16 to 20

Raspberry Sour Cream Coffee Cake with Raspberry Butter

THE INN AT BRANDYWINE FALLS, NORTHFIELD
INNKEEPER KATIE HOY

This moist and sweet coffee cake is a Sunday favorite at The Inn at Brandywine Falls, namesake of nearby sixty-seven-foot Brandywine Falls in Cuyahoga Valley National Park. The bed and breakfast is on the National Register of Historic Places and was built in 1848. Innkeepers George and Katie Hoy enjoy sharing stories with guests at breakfast, and they collected their favorites in a book along with their most popular recipes.

For the raspberry butter:
Line a 7½ x 3½-inch loaf pan (or other small loaf pan) with plastic wrap.

In a large bowl, beat the butter with a sturdy wooden spoon or electric mixer just until smooth.

Force the raspberries through a fine wire mesh strainer into a small bowl (a metal serving spoon works well). Discard the solids in the strainer. Add the resulting puree to the bowl with the butter and beat until combined. Scrape into the lined pan, smooth the top, and cover with more plastic wrap. Refrigerate. If you don't plan on using the butter within 2 days, cut it into smaller portions, wrap individually, and freeze.

For the raspberry sour cream coffee cake:
Preheat the oven to 350 degrees with a rack in the center. Spray a 10-inch Bundt pan with baking spray.

Sift together the flour, baking powder, and salt in a medium bowl. Set aside.

In a small bowl, mix the brown sugar, pecans, and cinnamon. Set aside.

In the bowl of an electric mixer, beat the raspberry butter and sugar until light, about 5 minutes. Add the eggs one at a time, scraping down the sides of the bowl with a rubber spatula after each addition. Beat in the sour cream. Add the flour mixture and mix just until blended (do not overmix).

Spoon a 1-inch layer of batter into the prepared pan. Sprinkle with one-third of the pecan-cinnamon mixture, and scatter one-third of the raspberries on the batter. Repeat two more times, ending with a thin layer of batter. Bake until a wooden skewer inserted in the center of the cake comes out clean, about 1 hour. Cool on a wire rack for 10 minutes, then invert onto the rack and cool for 30 minutes. Dust with powdered sugar before serving, if you like, and slather generously with raspberry butter.

Note: *If fresh raspberries are unavailable, substitute 6 ounces of frozen red raspberries, partially thawed. Substitute plain unsalted butter for the raspberry butter if you don't have any on hand.*

2½ pounds boneless pork butt

2 teaspoons kosher salt

1 tablespoon brown sugar

½ teaspoon freshly grated nutmeg

¼ teaspoon cayenne pepper

¼ teaspoon red pepper flakes

2 teaspoons ground dried sage

1½ teaspoons freshly ground
  black pepper

1½ teaspoons fresh thyme leaves,
  finely chopped

½ teaspoon fresh rosemary leaves,
  finely chopped

½ cup dry red wine, chilled

Vegetable oil for cooking

Makes 24 to 26 sausages

❧ **Note:** *If you don't have a meat grinder, you can have a good butcher grind 2½ pounds of pork butt for you. Despite its name, the butt is the thicker part of the shoulder typically with more marbling (fat). To freeze the shaped patties, place the lined tray in the freezer until the patties are firm, about 2 hours. Wrap in plastic, then foil. Sausages will keep in the freezer for 6 months. Thaw before cooking. You may also freeze the cooked patties.*

Sage Breakfast Sausage

RENNICK MEAT MARKET, ASHTABULA .
CHEFS ALEX ASTEINZA AND JENNIFER POCIASK

Rennick Meat Market pulls off a cosmopolitan feel in small-town Ashtabula's wine country. The space itself is a former butcher shop, so it's natural they'd make their own breakfast sausage, robust with red wine and fresh herbs. You can make a batch of this and freeze patties for special weekend breakfasts at home.

Cut the pork butt into cubes that will easily fit into your meat grinder (no larger than 2 inches). In a large bowl, combine the pork with the salt, sugar, spices, and herbs. Cover and refrigerate for 2 hours, or overnight.

Remove the meat mixture from the refrigerator. Using the finest die on the grinder, grind the meat into the mixing bowl of a stand mixer.

Using the paddle attachment, mix the ground meat on low, adding the red wine in a trickle as the mixer runs. Mix for about 2 minutes. The mixture should cling to itself and feel sticky—if not, run a few minutes longer (undermixed sausage will cook up with a mealy texture).

To check the seasoning, take about 1 tablespoon of the mixture and form into a small patty. Fry the patty in a small skillet filmed with oil until cooked through. Let cool a bit, then taste. Adjust seasoning to your liking, if necessary.

Line a baking sheet with parchment paper. With dampened hands to keep the mixture from sticking, form into patties 2½ to 3 inches across (about 2 ounces each) and place on the prepared sheet.

To cook, heat 2 to 3 teaspoons of vegetable oil in a heavy-bottomed skillet over medium heat. Add the sausage (don't crowd the pan) and cook, flipping every few minutes, until the outsides are nicely browned and the centers are no longer pink, 8 to 12 minutes.

Vanilla and lemon poached pears

4 firm pears

1 vanilla bean

1 tablespoon black peppercorns

1 cinnamon stick

½ teaspoon whole cloves

Juice of 3 lemons

Strips of zest from 2 lemons

⅔ cup sugar, plus more if needed

2 cups sweet white wine or water

1 tablespoon vanilla extract

Oatmeal

1 ½ cups water

½ cup Scottish oats
   (such as Bob's Red Mill)

Pinch salt

2 tablespoons dried currants

2 tablespoons dried cranberries

To serve

2 tablespoons chopped
   toasted pecans

2 tablespoons coconut flakes,
   toasted or plain

½ teaspoon sesame seeds

Unsweetened almond or rice milk

Serves 2

Scottish Oats with Vanilla and Lemon Poached Pears

ARTHUR MORGAN HOUSE, YELLOW SPRINGS
CHEF ERIN CAMPBELL

The lemony zip of these poached pears lends the comforting warmth of oat porridge an enlivening spin. Scottish oats are similar to steel-cut oats, but they are cut smaller and cook faster. Poach the pears in advance and cook the oats as you brew your morning coffee, and you have a special-occasion breakfast with minimal hands-on cooking time.

For the vanilla and lemon poached pears:
Peel, halve, and core the pears. Split the vanilla bean vertically and scrape the seeds out with a paring knife. Place the pears in a large saucepan with the vanilla bean and seeds, spices, lemon juice and zest, sugar, and wine or water. Add enough water, if necessary, so the liquid just covers the pears. Stir gently, cover, and bring to a boil. Reduce the heat to a simmer and gently cook until the pears are easily pierced with a knife, about 30 minutes.

With a slotted spoon, transfer the pears to a bowl and allow to cool slightly. Bring the poaching liquid back to a boil and simmer until it's syrupy, about 5 to 10 minutes. Add the vanilla extract and taste; if you used water and not the sweet wine, you'll probably want to add 2 to 3 more tablespoons of sugar.

Slice the poached pears into ½-inch wedges and return to the pan with the poaching liquid. Cover to keep warm until the oatmeal is ready.

(continued on page 26)

For the oatmeal:

Pour the water into a medium saucepan, then add the oats, salt, and dried fruit. Bring to a boil over medium–high heat, reduce the heat to medium–low, and cook, stirring frequently, for about 10 minutes. The oats are done when they have a slightly chewy texture.

To serve:

Divide the oats between two large bowls and top with a few warm poached pear slices. Spoon a bit of the poaching liquid over oats and garnish with toasted pecans, coconut flakes, and sesame seeds. Serve with unsweetened almond or rice milk.

Appetizers & Snacks

Ahi Tuna Tartare with Crispy Wontons and Meyer Lemon Aioli, p. 28

Tartare

1 ½ tablespoons pine nuts

4 ounces sushi-grade ahi tuna, finely chopped

1 tablespoon finely diced red and yellow sweet peppers

1 tablespoon thinly sliced fresh chives

½ teaspoon black sesame seeds

1 teaspoon toasted sesame oil

½ teaspoon habanero oil or chili oil (optional)

¼ teaspoon kosher salt

Freshly ground black pepper

Meyer lemon aioli

1 Meyer lemon

3 garlic cloves, minced

½ cup extra-virgin olive oil

½ cup vegetable oil

Dash freshly ground white pepper

Salt

Ahi Tuna Tartare with Crispy Wontons and Meyer Lemon Aioli

BEAU'S ON THE RIVER, CUYAHOGA FALLS
CHEF BILLY THURMAN

Perched dramatically over rapids on the Cuyahoga River, Beau's on the River draws diners with more than its view. Impressive to look at, this tower of tuna is a lot easier to pull together than you might think.

For the tartare:
Put the pine nuts in a small, dry skillet over medium heat. Cook, shaking the pan often, until the pine nuts are fragrant and golden brown (be careful—pine nuts burn very easily). Immediately remove from heat and put in a medium bowl to cool.

Combine the tuna, bell peppers, chives, sesame seeds, oils, salt, and pepper in the bowl with the pine nuts and gently mix. Refrigerate.

For the Meyer lemon aioli:
Zest the lemon with a microplane grater and reserve the zest. Juice the lemon into a medium bowl and add the garlic. Whisking constantly, add the oils in a thin stream until a creamy, opaque mayonnaise forms. Add the reserved lemon zest, white pepper, and salt to taste.

For the wontons and assembly:
Line a plate with paper towels. Heat about 2 cups of oil in a medium saucepan to 350 degrees. Gently lay one or two wonton wrappers at a time in the oil and fry until golden, flipping halfway through, about 1 minute total. Remove from the oil with a slotted spoon and lay on the paper towels to drain. (Wontons may be fried up to 2 weeks in advance and stored in an airtight container.)

To assemble, smear a few dabs of aioli decoratively down the center of the serving plate. Put a third of the tartare in the center, then a small dollop of aioli and a few radish slices. Top with a wonton, another third of the tartare, and more radish slices. Repeat once more.

Wontons and assembly

Vegetable oil, for frying

8 purchased wonton wrappers

2 radishes, very thinly sliced

1 orange, for zesting

½ cup micro arugula
  or other micro greens

Serves 2

Put a final wonton on top, then zest the orange over the wonton stacks. Garnish with the micro arugula and serve immediately.

❧ **Note:** *Crispy wontons are fun to snack on. It's a good idea to fry extra. If you prefer not to make your own aioli from scratch, dress up prepared mayonnaise with some minced garlic and finely grated lemon zest. Squeeze in a little juice to thin it out and add some zip.*

(see photograph on page 27)

2 pounds baby potatoes (ideally 1 to 2 inches in diameter)

½ cup (1 stick) unsalted butter, diced

½ cup milk, warmed

Salt and freshly ground black pepper

1 tablespoon minced fresh parsley

3 ounces (¾ cup) grated white Cheddar cheese, divided

Vegetable oil, for frying

Serves 10

Baby Twice-Baked Potatoes with Herbs and Cheese

THE CULINARY VEGETABLE INSTITUTE, MILAN
EXECUTIVE CHEF LIAISON JAMIE SIMPSON

These crowd-pleasers can be made in advance before serving as hors d'oeuvres. But be sure to let them cool a bit before offering to guests. "These little potatoes are like napalm right out of the oven," says Simpson, who also likes to serve them as a side to a meal.

Preheat the oven to 325 degrees.

Wash and dry the potatoes. Set on a rimmed baking sheet and bake until tender, about 40 minutes. Remove from the oven. Once cool enough to handle, cut the top edge off the potatoes with a paring knife. Hollow out carefully using a small measuring spoon or melon baller, reserving the flesh. Set the shells aside.

Place the potato flesh in a small saucepan over low heat. Mash until smooth. Mash in the butter one cube at a time until fully incorporated. Add just enough milk for a consistency that's creamy and fluffy, not soupy (you may not need all the milk). Season to taste with salt and pepper. Fold in parsley and ½ cup of the cheese. Let cool.

Line a rimmed plate with paper towels. In a large saucepan, heat at least 3 inches of vegetable oil to 325 degrees. Carefully add the reserved potato shells in batches and fry until very crispy and golden brown, about 5 minutes. Remove from the oil with a slotted spoon and lay on the paper towels to drain (hot oil will pool in the cavities of the potato shells, so make sure the open sides face down).

Spoon the cooled mashed potato filling into a heavy-duty quart zip-top bag. Snip off the tip of one corner. Pipe the filling into the crispy shells. Top with the remaining ¼ cup grated cheese. Cover and refrigerate until needed.

To serve, preheat the oven to 325 degrees. Set the potatoes on a rimmed baking sheet and bake until the filling is hot and the tops are golden brown, about 15 minutes.

¼ cup warm water

2 teaspoons brown sugar

1 scant tablespoon active dry yeast
(one ¼-ounce package)

4¼ cups bread flour

2 teaspoons salt

1 tablespoon diastatic malt powder
(optional)

1 cup plus 6 tablespoons
(11 fluid ounces) warm water

2½ tablespoons salted butter,
melted

¼ cup baking soda

Coarse salt, for sprinkling

Makes about 18 pretzels

Brewfontaine Signature Pretzels

BREWFONTAINE, BELLEFONTAINE
HEAD BAKER HANNAH WISCHMEYER

Brewfontaine's popular mustache-shaped pretzels invite goofy mugging and are as fun to make as they are to eat. Warm and crusty, they are a great vehicle for beer cheese or mustard (Brewfontaine serves them with Saucy Sows sweet pepper mustard made in Jackson Center) and are the perfect foil for one of the brewpub's beers. Diastatic malt powder, which improves the dough's ability to rise and brown, is the secret weapon to elevating these from ordinary homemade pretzels.

In a small glass measuring cup, whisk together the warm water and sugar. Mix in the yeast and set aside until the yeast is dissolved and foamy, about 5 minutes.

Measure the flour, salt, and diastatic malt powder (if using) in the bowl of a stand mixer fitted with a dough hook. With the mixer running on low, add the proofed yeast, additional warm water, and melted butter. Mix on low speed for 5 minutes; the dough should be smooth and supple. Add a little more water or flour, if necessary, to achieve the right consistency. Remove the dough from the mixer and knead by hand for a minute or so, then place in a greased bowl, cover with plastic wrap, and let rise until doubled, 30 minutes to 2 hours.

As the dough rises, prepare the baking soda. Preheat the oven to 250 degrees. Put the baking soda on a pie plate and cover with foil. Bake for 1 hour. Cool, then sift to break up any lumps. Set aside.

When the dough is doubled, gently deflate it. Preheat the oven to 375 degrees with racks in the upper and lower thirds of the oven. Line two baking sheets with parchment.

(continued on page 32)

Divide the dough into eighteen pieces, each about 3 ounces. With your hands, roll each one into a snake about 10 inches long and tapered on the ends. Roll each end up a bit to form a mustache, then lay on the prepared baking sheet. Repeat with remaining dough. Let rise until nearly doubled, 30 to 60 minutes.

Bring 8 cups of water to boil in a large saucepan or stockpot. Add the baking soda and stir until dissolved. Reduce the heat to a simmer. One or two at a time, gently lower the mustaches into the water for 10 seconds on each side. Remove with a slotted spoon and return to the baking sheet. Sprinkle with the coarse salt and bake until dark brown, 20 to 25 minutes. Serve warm, with mustard or beer cheese.

Leftover pretzels will keep in a bag for a day or so. Warm in a 350–degree oven for 5 minutes before eating.

❧ **Note:** *At Brewfontaine they use a solution of food-grade lye to get the classic pretzel look, but a baking soda solution is easier to work with and produces good results for a home cook. Diastatic malt helps the dough rise and produces a nice brown crust.*

Driftwood Steamed Mussels

WOLF'S RIDGE BREWING, COLUMBUS
EXECUTIVE CHEF SETH LASSAK

Known for its food as much as its microbrewed beers, Wolf's Ridge Brewing takes pub fare to a new level of execution and creativity. Chef Lassak's seafood dishes, in particular, are a highlight. His riff on mussels steamed in beer gets a robust boost from Spanish chorizo. Don't skip the baguette, since you'll want to mop up as much of the buttery, garlicky sauce as possible. Lassak recommends enjoying this with Wolf's Ridge Brewing Driftwood IPA.

2 pounds fresh mussels

¼ cup extra-virgin olive oil

1 cup sliced yellow onion
  (about 1 medium onion)

¼ cup minced garlic (from 1 head)

Kosher salt and freshly ground
  black pepper

4 ounces dry-cured Spanish chorizo,
  thinly sliced

1 cup Wolf's Ridge Brewing
  Driftwood IPA, or any craft-
  brewed session IPA

¾ cup (1¼ sticks) unsalted butter,
  diced

¼ cup minced flat-leaf parsley

1 baguette, cut on a deep bias
  into ½-inch slices

1 lemon, cut into wedges

Himalayan pink salt, for finishing

Serves 4 as a starter, 2 as a main dish

Place the mussels on ice to keep them cold. Scrub any grit or debris off their shells and pull out the beard, if any. Rinse the de-bearded mussels in cold water and set on a fresh bowl of ice.

In a large Dutch oven over medium heat, add the olive oil. When it shimmers, add the onion and garlic and cook until softened, about 2 minutes. Season lightly with salt and pepper. Add the mussels and increase the heat to high. Stir constantly for 2 minutes. Add the chorizo and cook for 2 more minutes, stirring constantly.

Add the beer and cover. Cook for 4 to 6 minutes, uncovering every minute or so to stir. Once the mussels start to open, remove the lid. Add the butter, one cube at a time, shaking the pot a bit so it emulsifies into a sauce. Sprinkle in the parsley and season to taste with salt and pepper.

While the mussels cook, heat a grill pan over medium-high heat. Grill the baguette slices until charred a bit on both sides.

Mound the mussels up in a big serving bowl. With a ladle, pour the brothy sauce over them. Garnish with a lemon wedge and slices of the grilled baguette. Finish with a sprinkle of Himalayan salt and serve.

❧ **Note:** *If you can't find bottled Wolf's Ridge Brewing IPA, any good session IPA—one that's not too heavily hopped—will do.*

Filling

3 ears fresh sweet corn

8 ounces fresh chèvre

¼ cup minced shallot

1 tablespoon finely chopped
cilantro, fennel fronds,
or other fresh leafy herbs

¼ teaspoon kosher salt

Freshly ground black pepper

15 to 20 male zucchini blossoms
with stem, each about the size
of your thumb

Cooking and garnish

Vegetable oil, for frying

2½ cups tapioca flour
or all-purpose flour, divided

1 cup club soda or sparkling water

2 teaspoons honey, preferably
local and raw, for drizzling

Serves 6 to 8 as an appetizer

Fried Stuffed Costata Romanesco Zucchini Blossoms

MICHAEL ANTHONY'S AT THE INN, VERSAILLES
CHEF MICHAEL A. DELLIGATTA

Chef Delligatta and his wife, Telisa, run Michael Anthony's at the Inn, where their menu changes seasonally. With its fresh corn and delicate squash blossoms, this appetizer is the epitome of summertime. Savory, sweet, creamy, and crunchy all at once, these fried squash blossoms beg to be devoured. A drizzle of honey makes their flavors really pop. For the lightest and crispiest batter, use tapioca flour. Also, pick the blossoms early in the day while the flowers are still open.

For the filling:
Cut the kernels off the ears of corn. In a large bowl, beat the chèvre a bit to loosen it, then fold in the corn kernels, shallots, herbs, and salt and pepper. Taste and adjust seasonings to your liking with more salt or pepper. (You may make the filling a day or two in advance.)

Transfer the filling to a large pastry bag fitted with a tip wide enough for the corn kernels to pass through. (If you don't have a pastry bag, use a quart zip-top freezer bag and snip off the corner.) Carefully insert the tip into a blossom and pipe in the filling. Do not overfill. Repeat until all the blossoms are filled. (You may fill the blossoms a day in advance; set on a plate, cover with plastic wrap, and refrigerate.)

To cook and garnish:
To fry the blossoms, line a large plate with paper towels and set aside. Put 1 cup of the flour in a wide, shallow bowl and set aside. Pour oil to a depth of 1½ to 2 inches in a large cast-iron skillet or Dutch oven and heat to 375 degrees.

While the oil heats, make the tempura batter by combining the remaining 1½ cups flour with the club soda or sparkling water.

Whisk together to form a batter that's about the consistency of heavy cream (not thick like pancake batter). Add a little more flour or club soda, if necessary.

Dredge a filled blossom in the plate of flour, then dip into the batter. Gently set the blossom into the hot oil and fry for about 45 seconds. Turn it over and fry until golden brown, about 15 seconds more. Remove from the oil with a slotted spoon or skimmer and place on the paper towels to drain. Repeat with the remaining blossoms (it's easier to fry only a few at a time).

Place the fried, drained blossoms on a plate, drizzle with the honey, and serve immediately.

• **Note**: *Depending on the size of the blossoms, you may have some leftover filling. It goes wonderfully tossed with a little hot cooked pasta.*

Crab cakes

½ teaspoon Old Bay seasoning

1 scallion, sliced thinly on the bias

1 large egg, slightly beaten

½ teaspoon freshly squeezed
 lemon juice

1 tablespoon whole grain mustard

¼ teaspoon Tabasco™ sauce

½ teaspoon minced fresh parsley

⅛ teaspoon freshly ground
 black pepper

¼ cup panko bread crumbs

¼ cup mayonnaise

1 pound jumbo lump crab meat,
 drained and picked over

Verde tartar sauce

½ cup mayonnaise

1½ teaspoons sweet pickle relish

1½ teaspoons freshly squeezed
 lemon juice

1½ teaspoons finely chopped
 fresh parsley

½ teaspoon Tabasco™ sauce

½ teaspoon Worcestershire sauce

1 teaspoon capers, rinsed,
 patted dry, and roughly
 chopped

Jumbo Lump Crab Cake Sliders

THE TWISTED OLIVE, NORTH CANTON
EXECUTIVE CHEF JERRY RISNER

Saucy and colorful, these sliders make a great main course or starter. You can opt to serve them without the bun, if you prefer, and instead plate them on a small bed of arugula leaves.

For the crab cakes:
Combine all the ingredients except the crab meat in a large bowl; mix well. Cover and refrigerate for 15 minutes. With your hands, gently fold in the crab meat. Form into twelve cakes. Lay on a parchment-lined baking sheet and chill to firm up while you make the sauces.

For the verde tartar sauce:
In a small bowl, thoroughly mix all the ingredients. Refrigerate until needed.

For the spiced mango sauce:
Place the mango chutney in a small food processor and pulse until smooth. Transfer to a small bowl and stir in the chile sauce. Refrigerate until needed.

To cook and assemble the crab cakes:
In a large skillet, melt the butter over medium-high heat. Add the crab cakes and sauté until golden brown, 3 to 5 minutes per side (you may need to do this in batches).

Spread 1½ teaspoons of the spiced mango sauce on each bottom bun and top with a crab cake. Spread 1½ teaspoons of the verde tartar sauce on the top bun, followed by three or four arugula leaves and a slice of Roma tomato. Serve immediately.

Spiced mango sauce

½ cup mango chutney

¼ cup Thai sweet chile sauce
(such as May Ploy)

To cook and assemble

4 tablespoons unsalted butter

12 slider buns, split and lightly
toasted

2 Roma tomatoes, thinly sliced

1 cup loosely packed
arugula leaves

Makes 12 sliders

½ cup finely diced red onion

2 tablespoons roughly chopped
fresh cilantro, stems included

2 tablespoons plus 1 teaspoon
freshly squeezed lime juice

¼ teaspoon cumin

¼ teaspoon fine sea salt

1 habanero pepper, seeded
and minced (see Note)

2 cups pitted ripe stone fruit
cut into ½-inch chunks

Makes 2 cups

Orchard Habanero Salsa

CASA NUEVA RESTAURANT AND CANTINA, ATHENS
FOOD COORDINATOR AL SCHMIDT

The floral character and sophisticated heat of habanero peppers comple-ments the succulence of ripe fruit in this tangy-sweet salsa. It's especially good made with stone fruit such as plums, nectarines, or peaches. This salsa is a smart use for blemished fruit that's a little soft, but not over the hill. Besides the obvious—corn chips—try this on grilled chicken, salmon, tuna, or shrimp.

Combine all the ingredients in a food processor and pulse until chunky but not pureed. Part of the appeal of this salsa is having pieces of fruit in different sizes to give it an interesting texture. Dip a chip in the salsa and taste for seasoning, then serve. Salsa will keep, covered and refrigerated, for about 3 days.

☙ **Note:** *Unless the skins are especially leathery or fuzzy, there's no need to peel the fruit. To avoid burns from capsaicin, wear rubber gloves when handling the habanero pepper and don't touch your face until you've removed the gloves and thoroughly washed your hands.*

¼ cup warm water

1 scant tablespoon active dry yeast
  (one ¼-ounce package)

3¼ cups all-purpose flour,
  divided

1 teaspoon salt

4 tablespoons unsalted butter,
  divided

2 tablespoons honey

¾ cup buttermilk

1 large egg

8 to 9 ounces thinly sliced
  pepperoni

Makes 12 rolls

Pepperoni Rolls

SARA BIR, THE SAUSAGETARIAN

They may be the official state snack food of West Virginia, but you'll find pepperoni rolls all along Ohio's southeast and northeast regions. A soft and cottony dough encases sticks or slices of pepperoni, and the grease renders out during baking to enrich the roll, leaving telltale streaks of reddish-orange. Pepperoni roll lovers passionately dispute the superiority of sticks versus slices. Some versions have cheese on or in the roll; some are even served with tomato sauce. Originally created as a filling lunch or snack for coal miners, they hit the spot wherever you may be.

Place the warm water in a small bowl and sprinkle the yeast over it. Let it sit until dissolved and silky, about 5 minutes.

Meanwhile, in the bowl of an electric stand mixer fitted with the dough hook, combine 3 cups of the flour and the salt.

In a small saucepan, melt 2 tablespoons of the butter over medium-low heat. Whisk in the honey and buttermilk and heat just until warm to the touch (do not boil). Remove from heat and beat in the egg.

Add the water and yeast mixture to the flour, and then add the buttermilk mixture. Mix on low speed until the dough just comes together. If it's quite sticky, add the remaining ¼ cup flour. Mix on low for 5 minutes, then remove the dough from the mixer and knead by hand until the dough is smooth and supple, another minute or so. Place in a greased bowl, cover, and let rise in a warm place until doubled in bulk, 1 to 2 hours.

Preheat the oven to 350 degrees with racks in the upper and lower thirds of the oven. Divide the dough into twelve equal pieces and let rest on a lightly floured board for 10 minutes.

(continued on page 40)

Line two baking sheets with parchment. Melt the remaining
2 tablespoons butter.

Take one piece of dough and form into a square roughly 4 to 5
inches across (imperfection is totally acceptable here, maybe even
preferable). Shingle nine slices of pepperoni over the square, leaving
a ¼-inch border. Roll up and pinch the seam lightly to seal. Place
seam side down on the baking sheet. Repeat with the remaining
dough, setting six rolls per sheet.

Brush the rolls with half the melted butter and let rise for 30 minutes
(the rolls will not puff up visibly). Bake until lightly browned, 30 to
40 minutes, rotating the sheets from top to bottom and back to front
halfway through baking. Immediately brush with the remaining
butter. Serve warm or at room temperature.

Pickled Blueberries

MALABAR FARM RESTAURANT, LUCAS
CHEF JOSEPH MOTTER AND SOUS CHEF SIERRA CARVER

Malabar Farm State Park was home to Pulitzer Prize–winning author Louis Bromfield, who originated the concept of conservation farming. He ran it as a working farm, which became a national example of sustainable agriculture. Malabar Farm Restaurant uses products grown on the farm, such as the blueberries in this simple but addictive pickle. Try them on salads, on top of a grilled steak, or just snack on a few straight from the fridge; they're surprisingly refreshing.

1 cup red wine vinegar

¼ cup sugar

1 teaspoon kosher salt

3 cups (1 pound) fresh blueberries

Makes about 4 cups

In a 4-cup glass measuring cup or medium non-reactive bowl, whisk together the vinegar, sugar, and salt until dissolved. Add the blueberries to the pickling liquid, cover, and refrigerate for at least 24 hours.

You may either keep the blueberries in the bowl or transfer them to a sterilized quart jar or two pint jars. Refrigerated in their brine, the blueberries will keep up to 4 months. You can also process them in a water bath canner and store at a cool temperature for up to 2 years.

8 hard-boiled eggs,
    peeled and halved

¼ cup mayonnaise

¼ cup finely chopped Tony Packo's
    Pickles & Peppers

1 teaspoon yellow mustard

Paprika or fresh chives,
    for garnish (optional)

Serves 8 to 16

Pickles & Peppers Deviled Eggs

TONY PACKO'S, TOLEDO

A Toledo institution, Tony Packo's has been serving hearty Hungarian-inspired food since 1932. They also sell a line of jarred "Pickles & Peppers" that has a deserved cult following. These simple but addictive deviled eggs pack an appealing crunch from the pickles and peppers.

Remove the yolks from the eggs and place in a small mixing bowl. Mash thoroughly with a fork. Add the mayonnaise, chopped pickles and peppers, and mustard and beat until smooth.

Spoon or pipe the filling into the center of the cooked egg halves. Garnish with a tiny sprinkle of paprika or fresh chives, if you like. For maximum flavor, refrigerate at least 2 hours before serving.

❧ **Note:** *Tony Packo's also makes Sweet Hot Pickles & Peppers. If you like your food a little spicy, use these in the filling instead of the regular Pickles & Peppers.*

½ cup (1 stick) unsalted butter

½ cup finely diced onion

1 cup finely diced hot wax chiles
(seeded if you prefer less
spicy heat)

¼ teaspoon freshly ground
black pepper

8 ounces cream cheese, softened

1 (13½-ounce) can diced tomatoes,
with liquid

8 ounces (2 cups) coarsely
grated Monterey Jack cheese

Salt

Serves 6 to 8

Queso con Chiles Dip

CASA NUEVA, ATHENS & FOOD COORDINATOR AL SCHMIDT

*A longtime fixture in the thriving university town of Athens, Casa Nueva is
a worker-owned restaurant and bar that's a destination for the kind of relaxed,
chatty meals you may recall from your college days. Their addictively edible
tortilla chips are made by Shagbark Seed & Mill from Ohio-grown corn,
and they find their soul mate in this cheesy dip. Bring a batch to a party
and you'll be instantly popular.*

In a medium saucepan, melt the butter over medium heat. Add the
onions and chiles and cook until softened, 5 to 7 minutes. Stir in
the black pepper.

Reduce the heat to medium–low. Add the cream cheese in chunks
and stir until smooth, then add the tomatoes and stir until smooth.
Initially the mixture may look curdled, but don't worry—it'll all come
together if you are patient. Add the Monterey Jack cheese and stir
until completely melted. Taste and add salt, if necessary (depending
on the canned tomatoes you use, you may not need to).

Serve immediately, with chips. Leftovers may be refrigerated and
reheated gently on the stove.

Roasted Elotes (Mexican Sweet Corn with Spicy Aioli)

STIX RESTAURANT, FINDLAY　❧　CHEF RENZ SALANGA

Ohioans love their sweet corn with butter, salt, and pepper. For something different, throw some ears on the grill and fix them up Mexican style with a rich, fiery mayonnaise and crumbled Cotija cheese. Elotes are usually served as a snack or appetizer, so you can count on one ear per person—unless you are serving sweet corn fanatics, which is likely.

Light a gas or charcoal grill for direct grilling over high heat.

Spicy aioli

2 tablespoons hot pepper sauce (such as Tapatio™)

2 tablespoons grape seed oil or other neutral oil

4 to 5 roasted garlic cloves, peeled (*see Note*)

½ teaspoon kosher salt

¼ teaspoon freshly ground black pepper

½ cup mayonnaise

Elotes

8 ears corn, shucked

Smoked Spanish paprika or mild chili powder, for sprinkling

¼ cup finely crumbled Cotija cheese or finely grated Parmesan cheese

¼ cup roughly chopped fresh cilantro, for garnish

Lime wedges, for serving

Serves 4 to 8

For the spicy aioli:
As the grill heats, make the spicy aioli. In a mini food processor, puree the hot pepper sauce, oil, roasted garlic, salt, and pepper. Stir in the mayonnaise. Set aside.

For the elotes:
When the grill is hot, set the corn on the grates directly over the coals or flames and grill, turning every 2 minutes, until all sides are nicely charred, about 8 minutes total.

To serve, smear the aioli in a thin layer all over the corn. Sprinkle with the paprika or chili powder, then with the Cotija. Garnish with cilantro and serve with lime wedges on the side.

❧ ***Note:*** *You'll have leftover spicy aioli, but it's great on sandwiches or used in dressings—anywhere you'd like a nice kick. To roast garlic, preheat the oven to 400 degrees. Cut the very tops off one or more heads of garlic and rub a little olive oil on the cut surfaces. Wrap the garlic loosely in foil and roast until golden brown and very soft, 40 to 60 minutes.*

Thousand Island dressing

⅔ cup mayonnaise

1 teaspoon freshly squeezed
    lemon juice

1½ tablespoons ketchup

1 tablespoon capers, rinsed,
    patted dry, and chopped

½ cup minced dill pickle

¼ teaspoon freshly ground
    black pepper

Sauerkraut balls

1½ pounds russet potatoes,
    peeled and cut into 2-inch chunks

3 tablespoons unsalted butter

½ cup milk

Salt and freshly ground black pepper

12 ounces (about 2 cups) fresh
    sauerkraut, strained and
    roughly chopped

12 ounces (about 1½ cups)
    coarsely grated Swiss cheese

8 ounces deli corned beef,
    finely chopped

3 large eggs

2 cups fine dry bread crumbs

Vegetable oil, for frying

¼ cup Thousand Island dressing,
    for serving

Serves 10

Sauerkraut Balls

MECKLENBURG GARDENS, CINCINNATI
KITCHEN MANAGER JAMES BROWN

Piping hot and deep fried, sauerkraut balls are the supreme tavern food, the hush puppies of Ohio. Said to have originated in Akron, you can find them on menus across the state, including at Mecklenburg Gardens. The vast beir-garten has been serving hearty German food since 1865. Mashed potatoes make these kraut balls less dense than those bound with bread crumbs.

For the Thousand Island dressing:
In a small bowl, mix all the ingredients together until smooth.

For the sauerkraut balls:
In a medium saucepan, cover the potatoes with water. Season generously with salt. Bring to a boil, reduce to a simmer, and cook until tender. Drain, mash, and beat in the butter and milk. Season generously with salt and pepper. Cool slightly.

In a large bowl, combine the mashed potatoes, sauerkraut, cheese, and corned beef. With a sturdy wooden spoon or your hands, mix well. Form into ovals about 2 to 2½ inches long.

In a medium bowl, beat the eggs with 3 tablespoons water. Set the bread crumbs in another bowl. Dip the sauerkraut balls in the egg wash, then coat in bread crumbs. Set on a tray and refrigerate for at least 30 minutes.

Preheat the oven to 200 degrees. Line a tray with paper towels. Heat at least 3 inches of oil in a large, deep saucepan to 350 degrees. In batches, fry the sauerkraut balls until golden brown on the outside, 1 to 2 minutes. Remove from the oil with a slotted spoon and drain on the paper towels. Keep cooked sauerkraut balls warm in the oven as you fry the remaining ones.

Serve with Thousand Island dressing on the side.

❧ **Note:** *You can freeze the breaded, fried sauerkraut balls for up to 6 months. Bake in a preheated 375-degree oven for about 20 minutes to serve.*

Smoked Salmon Spread

THE REFECTORY RESTAURANT & BISTRO, COLUMBUS
CHEF RICHARD BLONDIN

A longtime Columbus fine-dining destination, The Refectory is housed in a former church built in 1853. Originally from Lyon, France, Chef Blondin serves classical French food with a contemporary twist, but this elegant appetizer spread is a throwback to the restaurant's early days in 1976. It unites both fresh and smoked salmon.

½ cup dry white wine

¼ cup minced shallot

4 ounces fresh salmon, boned and skinned

¾ cup (1½ sticks) unsalted butter, at room temperature

6 ounces smoked salmon, cut into very fine strips

1 tablespoon chopped fresh chives

1 tablespoon chopped fresh Italian parsley

Salt and freshly ground pepper

1 teaspoon freshly squeezed lemon juice

Serves 8 to 12

Bring the wine to boil in a small saucepan. Add the shallots and fresh salmon. Reduce the heat to a gentle simmer and poach for 2 minutes. Remove the pan from the heat, cover, and set aside for 5 minutes more.

Drain the poached salmon and the shallots from the wine and set aside to cool completely. Reserve the shallots but discard the wine.

In a large mixing bowl, beat the butter with a sturdy wooden spoon until smooth. Add the smoked salmon, chives, parsley, and the cooled poached salmon and shallots. Beat together until the mixture is smooth and spreadable (the fish will flake apart into smaller chunks). Season to taste with salt and pepper; add up to 1 teaspoon lemon juice if it tastes flat.

Pack into a decorative mold or airtight container. Serve with crackers or crostini. This spread will keep, tightly covered in the refrigerator, for 2 weeks.

1 tablespoon black peppercorns

1 tablespoon coriander seeds

1 tablespoon fennel seeds

1½ teaspoons crushed
    red pepper flakes

1 cup extra-virgin olive oil

1 tablespoon thyme leaves

Finely grated zest of 1½ oranges

12 ounces mixed olives
    of your choice

Cubed Manchego cheese,
    for serving

Makes 3 cups

Warm Marinated Olives and Manchego Cheese

SALAZAR, CINCINNATI   ❧   CHEF-OWNER JOSE SALAZAR

In Cincinnati's historical and happening Over-the-Rhine district, Salazar is similarly a mix of old and new. It's got the feel of a neighborhood hangout, where Chef Jose Salazar and his crew serve beautifully plated, ingredient-focused food. A little bowl of his orange-kissed olives is a great way to kick off a special dinner. These keep for a long time; make a batch to have on hand as a nibble for impromptu gatherings, or as "anytime" salty snacks.

Put the peppercorns, coriander, and fennel in a small skillet over medium heat and toast the spices until they are aromatic, 1 to 2 minutes. Transfer to a bowl and allow them to cool a bit.

Pound the seeds in a mortar and pestle until they are broken up somewhat, but not finely ground. Combine the seeds in a medium bowl with the red pepper flakes, olive oil, thyme, and orange zest. Cover and refrigerate at least overnight, and for up to 2 weeks.

To serve, gently heat up as many olives as you'd like with a little of the flavorful oil in a small skillet over medium heat. Transfer to a serving bowl and scatter with cubes of Manchego. Don't forget to set out an extra bowl for your guests' olive pits.

1 bunch (about 20) ramps,
    trimmed and cleaned

½ cup toasted walnuts

1 ounce (½ cup) finely grated
    Parmesan cheese

Salt and freshly ground black pepper

⅓ to ½ cup extra-virgin olive oil

Squirt freshly squeezed lemon juice

Makes about 1 cup

Wild Ramp Pesto

RURAL ACTION, THE PLAINS
CHESTERHILL PRODUCE AUCTION

The nonprofit Rural Action promotes economic, social, and environmental justice in southeast Ohio. Many of their projects involve agriculture and food, such as the Chesterhill Produce Auction, which gives small-scale farmers a place to sell their items. In the spring, foragers bring ramps (of the genus Allium) *to the auction. The allium, a touchstone of Appalachian cuisine and culture, has attained a cult status among foodies for its pungent, garlicky flavor. There's perhaps no better way to prepare a mess of ramps. For a vegan version, simply leave out the cheese.*

Cut the green leaves off the ramps, reserving the white stems and roots. Prepare an ice bath in a large bowl. Bring a medium sauce-pan of water to a rolling boil, add the ramp leaves, and cook for 15 seconds. Quickly transfer to the ice bath with a slotted spoon. When cool, drain the blanched leaves and pat dry with paper towels. (You can skip this blanching step, but it makes the pesto a brighter green.)

Combine the ramp leaves, stems, and roots in a food processor with the walnuts and pulse a bit to decrease the volume. Add the cheese and sprinkle with salt and pepper. With the processor running, slowly add the oil in a thin stream. Add enough so the pesto isn't too pasty but not so much that it gets runny; you'll have to eyeball it.

Taste (spread a dab of pesto on a crouton or crostini, if you can) and adjust the seasonings with salt, pepper, and lemon juice. Toss the pesto with cooked pasta, smear it on pizza dough as a topping, dress hot roasted potatoes with it, or just spread it on toasted crusty bread.

Store the pesto in a tightly sealed jar in the refrigerator for up to 2 weeks. You may also freeze the pesto in ice cube trays and transfer the frozen cubes to zip-top bags in your freezer for up to 3 months.

✖ **Note:** *To toast nuts, spread them on a rimmed baking sheet and toast in a preheated 350-degree oven until fragrant, about 5 minutes.*

Salads &
Sides

Honey Corn Muffins with Cacao Nibs, p. 56

1 cup all-purpose flour

1 tablespoon chili powder

½ teaspoon cayenne pepper

¼ teaspoon freshly ground
    black pepper

¼ teaspoon salt

3 large yellow onions, peeled
    and thinly sliced crosswise
    into rings on a mandoline

Vegetable oil, for frying

Serves 6 to 8

Cap City Fine Diner Chili Onion Rings

CAP CITY FINE DINER, GRANDVIEW AND GAHANNA
REGIONAL CHEF PETER CHAPMAN

Cap City serves these spicy onion rings with their meatloaf (see page 93 in Main Courses), but they go equally well with burgers, grilled chicken, barbecue ribs, or any other savory dish.

Sift together the flour, spices, and salt onto a large rimmed plate. Set aside.

Line a tray with paper towels. In a large, heavy-bottomed saucepan or Dutch oven, heat 3 inches of oil to 350 degrees.

Separate the onion slices into individual rings. Dredge in the seasoned flour, then shake off the excess using a wire mesh strainer. Carefully lay in a single layer in the oil. Fry until crispy and lightly browned, about 2 minutes. Remove from the oil with a skimmer and drain on the paper towels. Season with more salt and serve.

10 ounces (10 loosely packed cups) torn lettuce, such as iceberg, green leaf, romaine, or spring mix

2 teaspoons diced white onion

½ cup thinly sliced white mushrooms

¾ cup diced tomato

2 tablespoons dark raisins

½ cup crumbled feta cheese

½ cup grated mozzarella cheese

½ cup grated provolone cheese

1 cup diced grilled chicken breast

2 tablespoons crumbled cooked bacon

1 cup croutons

1 tablespoon finely grated Parmesan cheese

About 6 pita crisps, for garnish

Grumpy's Delicious Poppy Seed Dressing or other poppy seed dressing

Serves 2

Garbage Salad

GRUMPY'S DELI, TOLEDO
CHEF AND CO-OWNER JENNIFER SHEMAK

What's not in a Garbage Salad? This beloved jumble of everything tasty is a weekday lunch favorite at Grumpy's Deli in downtown Toledo. Every bite offers something salty, sweet, tart, and creamy. It's immensely satisfying and stealthily decadent, a big meal of a salad. Grumpy's bottles its house poppy seed dressing for retail sale, but if your local store doesn't carry it, any poppy seed dressing will do.

Divide the lettuce between serving bowls. Layer the vegetables, raisins, cheeses, chicken, and bacon over the lettuce. Scatter croutons and Parmesan on top, garnish with pita crisps, and serve immediately with the dressing on the side.

Cider vinegar granita

Half an English cucumber

1 ½ ribs celery, washed

½ cup filtered water

¼ cup apple cider vinegar

2 tablespoons honey

½ teaspoon kosher salt

Salad

1 head soft lettuce, such as Boston,
Bibb, or red leaf

6 to 12 radishes, thinly sliced
or quartered

Half a cucumber, thinly sliced

Pickled red onion (optional)

Extra-virgin olive oil, for drizzling

Coarse salt

Serves 12

Garden Salad with Cucumber, Celery, and Cider Vinegar Granita

THE CULINARY VEGETABLE INSTITUTE, MILAN
CHEF LIAISON JAMIE SIMPSON

Refreshing and simple, this tart-sweet shaved ice tops crunchy raw vegetables to make an unusual beginning to a meal on a hot day. It's a "set it and forget it" granita, with no bothersome need to periodically drag a fork through it as it freezes. Serve the granita on whatever garden-fresh vegetables are in season—the list here is just a suggestion. On its own, the granita has other uses, as well. Chef Simpson recommends it as a topping for oysters on the half shell.

For the cider vinegar granita:

Combine all the ingredients in a blender or food processor and puree until smooth. Pour into a Pyrex baking dish (a standard-size loaf pan works well) and cover with plastic wrap. Freeze until the juice is solid ice, at least 4 hours. Unmold and crush using the ice crush setting on a high-powered blender. You want to see some shards in the granita; it shouldn't be smooth like a slushie.

For the salad:

Arrange beds of lettuce leaves on serving plates (chilled ones are nice) and scatter the other vegetables over the lettuce. Top each salad with a spoonful of the granita, then drizzle each salad with a little olive oil and sprinkle with salt. Serve immediately.

❧ **Note:** *If you have them on hand, try adding a few Pickled Blueberries (see page 41 in Appetizers & Snacks) to the salad.*

3 large russet potatoes
(about 2½ pounds)

4 ounces bacon

1 small onion, chopped

1 tablespoon all-purpose flour

½ cup apple cider vinegar

1 cup water

½ cup brown sugar

1½ teaspoons kosher salt

½ teaspoon freshly ground
black pepper, divided

Serves 4

German Potato Salad

CLAY HAUS, SOMERSET ❧ OWNER SCOTT SNIDER

Sweet and sour, this potato salad is very old-fashioned in that the dressing is cooked and thickened with a bit of flour. It's an excellent side to sauerbraten, bratwurst, and sauerkraut, or most any hearty German fare—which is exactly what you'll find at the Snider family's charming restaurant. Somerset was settled by Pennsylvania Dutch, and the structure housing the restaurant was built between 1812 and 1820. President Andrew Jackson once dined in the front room. Today, diners at Clay Haus enjoy the historical photos and antiques lining the walls of the former private residence's various dining rooms.

Put the potatoes in a stockpot or large saucepan and add cold water to cover. Bring to a boil, reduce to a simmer, and cook until the potatoes are easily pierced with a fork but still hold their shape, 20 to 35 minutes. Drain. Once the potatoes are cool enough to handle, remove and discard the skins. Cut the cooked potato into slices about ¼ inch thick and place in a large heat-safe bowl. Set aside.

Meanwhile, lay the bacon in a skillet and set over medium-low heat. Cook, turning occasionally, until the bacon is browned and most of the fat is rendered out. Lay the bacon on a plate lined with paper towels and set aside.

Add the onions to the skillet, raise the heat to medium, and cook until translucent, about 10 minutes. Whisk in the flour, then add the vinegar, water, brown sugar, salt, and ¼ teaspoon of the black pepper. Bring to a boil and cook, whisking all the while, until the dressing is the consistency of a thin gravy, about 5 minutes.

Pour the hot dressing over the potatoes. Sprinkle the remaining ¼ teaspoon black pepper over the top, then crumble the cooked bacon into the bowl. Stir gently to combine. Serve warm.

❧ **Note:** *Potato cooking water makes a flavorful stock. If you like, reserve a cup of the potato stock before draining the potatoes and use it in the dressing instead of the water.*

Grilled Hearts of Romaine with Halloumi Cheese

SEASONS BISTRO AND GRILLE, SPRINGFIELD
CHEF DOUG MCGREGOR

Owned and operated by brother-sister team Margaret Mattox and Doug McGregor, Seasons brings refined dining to the small college town of Springfield, home of Wittenberg University. This is a perfect salad for summer dinners al fresco at the grill. If you've never had halloumi cheese, you're in for a treat. Salty and chewy, it's even better after a quick griddling in a hot skillet.

Caramelized onions

1 tablespoon unsalted butter

1 red onion, thinly sliced

1 tablespoon brown sugar

Balsamic vinaigrette

½ garlic clove, minced

½ teaspoon Dijon mustard

2 tablespoons balsamic vinegar

1 tablespoon maple syrup

6 tablespoons extra-virgin olive oil

Salt and freshly ground black pepper

Salad

8 ounces halloumi cheese,
    cut crosswise into 16 slices

2 hearts of romaine, cut in
    half lengthwise

Salt and freshly ground black pepper

Serves 4

For the caramelized onions:
In a medium skillet, melt the butter over medium heat. Add the onions and toss to coat. Add the brown sugar. Cook over medium–low heat, stirring occasionally, until onions are translucent and tender, about 20 minutes.

For the balsamic vinaigrette:
In a medium bowl, whisk together the minced garlic, Dijon, balsamic vinegar, and maple syrup. Slowly drizzle in the oil, whisking all the while. Season with salt and pepper to taste.

To build the salad:
Preheat a grill to medium–high heat.

Meanwhile, heat a large nonstick pan over medium–high heat. Add the halloumi slices and cook until a golden brown crust forms, 2 to 4 minutes per side. Remove from the pan and cover loosely to keep warm.

Place the romaine halves on the hottest part of the grill, cut side up. Sprinkle with salt and pepper. Grill until the outer leaves wilt and start to char, 30 seconds to 1 minute. Flip over and grill the other side until lightly charred.

Place the romaine hearts, face up, on plates. Top each with four slices of cheese, then some of the caramelized onions. Drizzle with dressing and serve immediately.

Cooking spray

2 tablespoons unsalted butter

2 tablespoons cacao nibs

½ cup organic cornmeal, preferably whole-grain

½ cup organic spelt flour

1 teaspoon baking powder

½ teaspoon salt

½ cup buttermilk

1 egg, beaten

3 tablespoons coconut sugar

About 1 tablespoon honey, divided

Makes 6 muffins

Honey Corn Muffins with Cacao Nibs

SHAGBARK SEED & MILL, ATHENS
CO-OWNER MICHELLE AJAMIAN

Shagbark mills Ohio-grown organic grains and processes dry beans sourced from small farmers in Ohio. Chefs throughout the state proudly offer Shagbark items on their menus. Shagbark's nutty spelt flour and robustly flavored cornmeal make these easy muffins stand out from similar quick breads. They're a little sweet, with a subtle fruitiness and exciting crunch from the cacao nibs. Serve them with chili, hearty stews, or on their own with a little jam and butter at breakfast.

Preheat the oven to 425 degrees with a rack in the center of the oven. Grease a standard-size six-cup muffin tin with cooking spray.

In a small saucepan, melt the butter over low heat. Stir in the nibs, then remove from heat and allow to steep.

Meanwhile, in a large bowl, whisk together the cornmeal, spelt flour, baking powder, and salt.

In a medium bowl, whisk together the buttermilk, egg, and coconut sugar until combined. Stir in the melted butter and nibs. Fold into the flour mixture with a rubber spatula just until a loose batter forms with no dry streaks.

Spoon the batter into the prepared tins. Put a small dollop of honey, about a ½ teaspoon or less, in the center of each tin of batter. Bake until the muffins are domed and a little brown at the edges, and a toothpick inserted in the center comes out free of crumbs, about 15 minutes. Remove muffins from the tins, cool on a wire rack for a minute or two, and serve warm. Leftover muffins are delicious split and toasted.

(see photograph on page 49)

1 tablespoon vegetable oil
    or bacon grease

1 small white onion, finely diced

1 teaspoon minced garlic

4 cups low-sodium chicken broth

1 cup quick-cooking grits

4 ounces (1 cup) grated white
    Cheddar cheese

½ cup sour cream

1 scallion, thinly sliced, divided

8 ounces bacon, cooked until
    crisp and crumbled, divided

Salt and freshly ground
    black pepper

Serves 4 to 6 as a side

Loaded Grits

CRAVE, AKRON EXECUTIVE CHEF LAURIE CRANO

Cooked grits make an ideal canvas for white Cheddar cheese, sour cream, and crumbled bacon. While fun to share as a side at dinnertime, they're also fantastic at breakfast.

In a medium saucepan, heat the oil or bacon grease over medium heat. Add the onions and cook until translucent, about 5 minutes. Add the garlic and cook for 1 minute. Add the chicken broth and bring to a boil. Slowly stir in the grits. Reduce the heat to medium–low and cook, stirring frequently, until creamy and thick, 5 to 8 minutes.

Remove from heat and stir in the Cheddar cheese and sour cream. Fold in three–quarters of the scallions and cooked bacon. Season to taste with salt and pepper. Garnish with the remaining bacon and scallions and serve.

2 tablespoons sugar,
   or more to taste

1 teaspoon kosher salt

⅓ cup mayonnaise

1 teaspoon dried dill

2 English cucumbers, peeled,
   halved, and sliced

6 scallions, thinly sliced

Juice of ½ lemon (optional)

Fresh dill, for garnish (optional)

Serves 6

Polish Cucumber Salad

SOKOLOWSKI'S UNIVERSITY INN, CLEVELAND
CO-OWNER MICHAEL SOKOLOWSKI

With its plentiful steam tables laden with classic Polish American cuisine, Sokolowski's has served Clevelanders of all stripes since 1923. Its solid execution of Eastern European comfort food earned a James Beard American Classics award in 2014. Serve this sweet and creamy yet refreshing salad with rich foods like the Potato and Cheddar Pierogi recipe (see page 114 in the Main Courses section). Cucumber salad is good at any time of year, but when well chilled, it really hits the spot on a hot summer day.

In a large bowl, combine the sugar, salt, mayonnaise, and dill and stir until the sugar is dissolved. Fold in the cucumbers and scallions. Taste and adjust seasoning, adding a squirt of lemon juice to brighten up the salad a bit, if you like. Chill for at least 30 minutes.

Right before serving, garnish with fresh dill.

2 large heads cauliflower,
    cut into 1- to 2-inch florets

¼ cup garlic-infused oil

Kosher salt and freshly ground
    black pepper

½ cup tahini paste

1 ½ teaspoons garlic power

2 to 3 tablespoons freshly
    squeezed lemon juice

¼ cup water

1 tablespoon fresh dill

Serves 4 to 6

Roasted Cauliflower

POCO PIATTI, PERRYSBURG   CHEF-OWNER ELIAS HAJJAR

Poco Piatti's menu focuses on Mediterranean small plates for sharing, such as this incredible roasted cauliflower in a creamy and tart tahini sauce. Members of Chef Elias Hajjar's family have been restauranteurs in the Toledo area for generations.

Preheat the oven to 425 degrees.

Combine the cauliflower and garlic oil in a large bowl. Season with salt and pepper to taste and toss to combine. Place on a rimmed baking sheet and roast until golden brown, 10 to 15 minutes.

Meanwhile, combine the tahini paste, garlic powder, lemon juice, and water in a medium bowl and whisk until smooth. Season to taste with salt. The tahini sauce should be thin but not runny; add a little more water or lemon juice to adjust the consistency, if needed.

Toss the hot cauliflower with enough tahini sauce to coat, then add the dill and toss once more. Serve immediately.

❧ **Note:** *If you have leftover tahini sauce, enjoy it on other roasted or grilled vegetables.*

2 roasted red or yellow
   bell peppers, skins, stems,
   and seeds discarded,
   cut into ½-inch dice (*see Note*)

4 medium Roma tomatoes,
   cut into ½-inch dice

1 English cucumber,
   cut into ½-inch dice

¼ cup thinly sliced red onion

¼ cup roughly chopped
   flat-leaf parsley

4 ounces (about ¾ to 1 cup)
   crumbled feta cheese

2 tablespoons extra-virgin olive oil

1 tablespoon apple cider vinegar

Salt and freshly ground
   black pepper

Serves 4

Shopska Salad

NASLADA BISTRO, BOWLING GREEN
CHEF-OWNER BOYKO MITOV

Chef Mitov and his wife, Mariana, moved to northwest Ohio from Bulgaria and eventually opened their bistro to share the foods they missed from their homeland. Naslada is the Bulgarian term for the sense of contentment that comes from a fine meal in good company. Their menu combines old world influences with a new world sensibility. This colorful salad, a Naslada Bistro fixture, goes well with a wide range of entrées.

Combine all the ingredients in a large bowl, season with salt and pepper to taste, toss, and enjoy immediately.

❧ **Note:** *To roast the peppers, set under a preheated broiler or grill on high heat, turning from time to time, until their skin is blistered and blackened all over. Place in a clean paper bag, fold the top over, and let rest for 10 minutes. Peel off the blackened skin and discard. If you prefer, you may use good-quality jarred roasted red bell peppers instead of roasting your own.*

4 tablespoons olive oil, divided

1 large yellow onion, diced

2 garlic cloves, minced

1 small eggplant with the skin on, cut in 1-inch cubes

1 teaspoon chopped fresh thyme leaves

1 yellow bell pepper, seeded and cut in 1-inch dice

1 red bell pepper, seeded and cut in 1-inch dice

2 small or 1 medium zucchini, sliced into ½-inch coins

6 Roma tomatoes, seeded and cut in 1-inch dice

2 tablespoons roughly chopped fresh basil

Kosher salt and freshly ground black pepper

1 tablespoon chopped fresh parsley

Makes about 6 cups

Simple Ratatouille

THE COOKING SCHOOL AT JUNGLE JIM'S INTERNATIONAL MARKET, FAIRFIELD ❧ CULINARY DIRECTOR LEIGH BARNHART OCHS

It may be one of the most famous Provençal dishes, but the summery jumble of vegetables that is ratatouille is perfect for Ohio, where most any avid gardener grows at least half the ingredients right in his or her own backyard. Make a batch and enjoy it on bruschetta, tossed with cooked pasta, topped with baked eggs, or as a vegetable side.

Heat 2 tablespoons of the oil in a 12-inch skillet over medium heat. Add the onions and cook, stirring occasionally, until softened, 5 to 6 minutes. Add the garlic and stir for 1 minute. Add the remaining 2 tablespoons oil and then the eggplant and thyme, and continue to cook, stirring occasionally, until the eggplant begins to soften, about 5 minutes.

Add the bell peppers and zucchini and continue to cook for 5 minutes. Add the tomatoes and basil. Sprinkle with salt and pepper to taste and cook for 5 minutes. Stir in the parsley and cook for 2 to 3 minutes, stirring occasionally. Serve warm or at room temperature.

¾ cup yellow cornmeal

1 cup plus 2 tablespoons
    all-purpose flour

¾ teaspoon baking powder

¾ teaspoon baking soda

1½ teaspoons kosher salt

1½ teaspoons sugar

1½ cups corn kernels,
    thawed if frozen

4 scallions, thinly sliced

2 cups buttermilk

4 tablespoons unsalted butter,
    melted and cooled

2 eggs, beaten

1½ teaspoons sambal or sriracha

¾ cup fresh bread crumbs
    (see Note)

Serves 4 to 8

Skillet Corn Cakes

MEADOWLARK RESTAURANT, DAYTON ❧ CHEF ELIZABETH WILEY

These delicious corn cakes are a staff favorite at Meadowlark. Freeze good sweet corn in the summer and make the corn cakes in the winter, serving them for brunch with bacon or sausages and eggs. Make them small as a base for appetizers or larger as a side—they're great with grilled salmon, pork, or even just crumbled bacon and diced tomato.

In a medium bowl, whisk together the cornmeal, flour, baking powder, baking soda, salt, and sugar.

In a large bowl, combine the corn, scallions, buttermilk, butter, eggs, and sambal or sriracha. Add the flour mixture and fold with a rubber spatula until combined, being careful not to overmix. Stir in the bread crumbs last.

Heat a nonstick electric griddle or large skillet to medium heat. Film with a bit of oil, then spoon on desired amounts of batter. Cook until the edges begin to set and bubbles form. Flip and cook through. Serve immediately.

❧ **Note:** *Make fresh bread crumbs by cutting several thick slices of good Italian or French bread. Cut off and discard the crust, tear the bread into small chunks, and pulse in a food processor into fluffy crumbs. This sturdy batter will hold for several days in the fridge, but if you prefer, you can easily halve it for a smaller yield.*

Dressing

¼ cup raspberry preserves

¼ cup apple cider vinegar

1 teaspoon dried mustard powder

½ teaspoon salt

½ teaspoon freshly ground
    black pepper

1 cup canola or sunflower oil

Spiced nuts

1 tablespoon unsalted butter

¼ teaspoon cinnamon

¼ teaspoon nutmeg

¼ teaspoon ground ginger

⅛ teaspoon cayenne

¼ teaspoon salt

1½ teaspoons sugar

1 cup pecan or walnut halves

Salad

8 cups mixed greens or
    baby spinach

1 quart strawberries, cleaned,
    hulled, and quartered

½ cup crumbled feta cheese

1 cup spiced walnuts or pecans

Serves 8

Strawberry Feta Salad with Raspberry Vinaigrette and Spiced Nuts

THE WHITE OAK INN, DANVILLE   ❧   INNKEEPER YVONNE MARTIN

Yvonne Martin is proud to be one of the blogging collective Eight Broads in the Kitchen, a group of innkeeper friends who share a passion for food and cooking. She created this lively salad, which offsets sweet strawberries with spicy, crunchy nuts and salty feta.

For the dressing:
Combine all the ingredients in a blender and puree until thoroughly blended. If necessary, add a little water so the dressing will drizzle well.

For the spiced nuts:
Preheat the oven to 350 degrees. Line a baking sheet with parchment paper.

Melt the butter in a medium saucepan. Stir in the cinnamon, nutmeg, ginger, cayenne, salt, and sugar. Add the nuts and stir to coat. Spread in a single layer on the prepared sheet. Bake for 15 to 20 minutes, stirring every 5 minutes. The nuts should be dark, but not scorched. Cool on the baking sheet, breaking clumps apart as soon as the nuts are cool enough to handle. Cool completely and store in an airtight container.

To assemble the salad:
Put 1 cup of greens on a plate. Sprinkle with the strawberries, feta cheese, and spiced nuts. Drizzle dressing over the top and serve immediately.

Summer Succotash

THE SEASONED FARMHOUSE, COLUMBUS
CHEF TRICIA WHEELER

Shelled fresh green soybeans take the place of the traditional lima beans in this classic American vegetable dish. A hint of bacon and cream temper the sweetness of the fresh corn and ripe tomatoes. It's the essence of summer, and very typical of the seasonally driven recipes that Chef Tricia Wheeler makes in classes at her recreational cooking school, The Seasoned Farmhouse, where visitors are greeted by raised beds full of herbs and vegetables.

3 to 4 slices bacon

1 tablespoon bacon fat or
    extra-virgin olive oil

1 medium red onion, diced

1 garlic clove, minced

1 large tomato, cored and diced

1 red pepper, diced

1 jalapeño, seeded and diced

6 ears fresh sweet corn,
    kernels shaved off the cob

1 cup shelled edamame,
    defrosted if frozen

3 to 4 tablespoons heavy cream

Salt and freshly ground
    black pepper

Serves 6 to 8

Lay the bacon in a heavy-bottomed skillet (preferably 12 inches) and cook slowly over medium heat until crisp. Drain on paper towels; crumble and set aside.

Pour off all but 1 tablespoon of the bacon fat from the skillet and increase the heat to medium-high. Add the onions, garlic, tomato, and peppers and sauté until soft, 3 to 5 minutes. Add the corn and edamame and cook, stirring frequently, until the corn chars a little, about 5 minutes.

Reduce the heat to medium, add the cream, and cook for 5 more minutes. The vegetables should still be a little firm and the cream will cling to them. Season to taste with salt and pepper. Garnish with cooked bacon and serve.

❧ **Note:** *To prepare this as a vegetarian dish, use olive oil and omit the bacon crumbles and drippings.*

2½ cups (20 ounces) sauerkraut

¼ cup canola oil

¼ cup apple cider vinegar

½ cup sugar

1½ cups finely diced celery

1 cup diced onion

⅓ cup finely diced green
bell pepper

Serves 8 to 12

Sweetkraut

SCHMIDT'S RESTAURANT AND SAUSAGE HAUS, COLUMBUS

A hybrid of slaw and an old-school sauerkraut salad, this will convert sauerkraut-haters and beguile sauerkraut-lovers. At Schmidt's, they serve it on the Mama Reuben sandwich, which features a giant slab of their spicy Bahama Mama sausage instead of corned beef. But sweetkraut is also good on grilled sausage or as a refreshing side salad at summer cookouts and potlucks.

Rinse the sauerkraut in a colander, squeezing out the excess liquid. Set aside.

Combine the oil, vinegar, and sugar in a large bowl. Beat with a large whisk until the dressing is uniform in color. Add the celery, onions, and bell pepper; continue to whisk until the dressing becomes a very pale green. Add the sauerkraut and mix well.

Refrigerate overnight to allow the flavors to blend. Serve chilled. Sweetkraut will keep, refrigerated, up to 2 weeks.

½ cup panko bread crumbs

2 tablespoons finely diced
    fresh tomato

2 teaspoons finely chopped
    fresh tarragon leaves

2 teaspoons unsalted butter, melted

8 ounces uncooked pasta shells

1½ cups heavy cream

4 ounces (1 cup) grated white
    Cheddar cheese

2 ounces (½ cup) grated
    Gouda cheese

2 ounces cream cheese, softened

¼ cup canned truffle peelings,
    drained (see Note)

Salt and freshly ground
    black pepper

Serves 6 as a side

Truffle Mac & Cheese

MANCY'S STEAKHOUSE, TOLEDO
CHEF MICHAEL ROSENDAUL

Luxury and comfort food meet in this over-the-top macaroni and cheese. Bountiful with cream and cheeses and studded with slices of black truffle, it's a far cry from the orange stuff that comes in a box. Chef Rosendaul uses goat milk Gouda from Turkeyfoot Creek Creamery in Wauseon, but regular Gouda works fine.

Preheat the oven to 350 degrees. Grease a 1½– to 2–quart baking dish.

In a small bowl, combine the bread crumbs, tomato, tarragon, and butter. Set aside.

Bring a large pot of salted water to a boil. Add the pasta and cook for 2 minutes less than suggested in the directions on the package, until still very toothy. Drain and return to the pot.

Meanwhile, in a large saucepan, bring the cream to a simmer over medium heat. Add the grated cheeses, cream cheese, and truffle peelings. Stir until melted and creamy. Season to taste with salt and pepper. (The sauce will be thin, but don't worry—the pasta will absorb liquid as it bakes.)

Pour the cheese sauce into the pot with the cooked pasta and stir until combined. Turn into the baking dish and sprinkle with the bread crumb mixture. Bake until bubbly and lightly browned, 20 to 30 minutes. Let sit for 10 minutes before serving.

✐ **Note:** *Truffle peelings are canned, sliced black truffles. They may be omitted.*

Cajun seasoning

2 teaspoons fine sea salt

2 teaspoons garlic powder

2½ teaspoons sweet paprika

1 teaspoon freshly ground
    black pepper

1 teaspoon onion powder

1 teaspoon cayenne pepper

1½ teaspoons dried oregano

1½ teaspoons dried thyme

Dirty rice

2 cups basmati rice

3 cups water

½ cup olive oil

1 medium onion, finely diced

3 ribs celery, finely diced

1 green bell pepper, seeded
    and finely diced

1 red bell pepper, seeded
    and finely diced

2 tablespoons chopped garlic

2 tablespoons Cajun seasoning,
    divided

Kosher salt

Serves 8 to 12

Vegan Dirty Rice

FUR PEACE RANCH, POMEROY   ❧   CHEF JUSTIN BERRY

Tucked away in the foothills of southeast Ohio, former Jefferson Airplane guitarist Jorma Kaukonen's retreat center, Fur Peace Ranch, offers work- shops for musicians of all levels. Guests eat at the spacious dining hall in two converted 150-year-old cabins. Accordingly, this recipe serves a crowd, but it's easy to halve the quantity. Enjoy this rice with red beans and sautéed vegetables.

For the Cajun seasoning:
Mix all the ingredients together and store in an airtight container. For optimal flavor, use within 6 months.

For the dirty rice:
In a medium saucepan, combine the rice and water. Cover, bring to a boil, reduce the heat to low, and cook until all the water is absorbed, about 20 minutes. Set aside to cool.

Heat the oil in a large, deep skillet or Dutch oven over medium heat. Add the onions, celery, and peppers and cook until the onions are translucent, 5 to 6 minutes. Add the garlic and cook for 2 minutes more. Add 1 tablespoon of the Cajun seasoning and stir until the ingredients are evenly coated.

Break apart the cooked rice with a fork so it's fluffy and not in clumps. Add the rice to the skillet, reduce the heat to low, and stir until the rice is evenly coated. Season to taste with more Cajun seasoning and salt, if needed. Remove from heat and serve.

❧ **Note:** *Store-bought Cajun seasonings vary a lot in salt levels. For the best Cajun flavor, blend your own with fresh spices, or look for a brand that does not have as much salt (you can always add more salt to taste).*

1 tablespoon aged balsamic
    vinegar

1 tablespoon extra-virgin olive oil

¼ teaspoon honey

¼ teaspoon kosher salt

⅛ teaspoon freshly ground
    black pepper

4 ounces extra-sharp white
    Cheddar cheese

4 cups loosely packed
    baby arugula

4 large leaves fresh basil,
    cut into thin shreds

2 cups red seedless grapes,
    halved

1 cup toasted pecans,
    roughly chopped

Serves 4 to 8

White Cheddar, Red Grape, and Toasted Pecan Salad

MOXIE, THE RESTAURANT, BEACHWOOD
CHEF JONATHAN BENNETT

A substantial first course, this salad is equally good served at the end of a meal. With generous helpings of nuts and fruit, it's like a small cheese course in salad form. Thin shreds of fresh basil add an unexpected punch of freshness.

Combine the vinegar, oil, honey, salt, and pepper in a medium mixing bowl; set aside.

Slice the cheese into thin cuts and then crumble into bite–size chunks. In a large bowl, toss the arugula and basil shreds with the dressing, then divide between plates. Garnish with grapes, cheese, and pecans and serve.

Soups & Stews

Avocado Bisque, p. 73

Croutons

2 tablespoons garlic powder

1 tablespoon onion powder

½ teaspoon dried parsley

½ teaspoon dried oregano

½ teaspoon dried thyme

1 teaspoon salt

½ loaf ciabatta bread, cut into
    ¾-inch cubes (6 cups cubed)

⅓ cup finely grated Parmesan
    or Romano cheese

⅓ cup extra-virgin olive oil

Soup

½ cup (1 stick) unsalted butter

3 large onions, thinly sliced

2 garlic cloves, chopped

Salt and freshly ground black pepper

½ cup ruby port

2 cups apple cider

4 cups low-sodium beef broth

1 sprig fresh thyme

2 apples, peeled, cored,
    and cut into ½-inch dice

To serve

2 cups croutons

8 ounces (2 cups) grated
    Gruyère cheese

Serves 6

Apple Onion Soup Gratinée

WHITE OAKS RESTAURANT, WESTLAKE   CHEF PETER KENDALL

White Oaks consistently lands on "most romantic" dinner destination lists. Their famous Apple Onion Soup is a close cousin of French onion soup. Apple cider, a splash of port, and tender diced apples give it a tangy sweetness that's a nice foil for the ooey-gooey crown of melted cheese.

For the croutons:
Preheat the oven to 425 degrees.

In a small bowl, stir together the garlic and onion powders, dried herbs, and salt. In a separate bowl, toss the bread cubes with the cheese, oil, and 1 tablespoon of the seasoning mixture. Spread on a rimmed baking sheet and bake until browned and crispy, 7 to 12 minutes, tossing halfway through the baking time. Let cool. Croutons will keep in a tightly sealed container for 1 month.

For the soup:
Melt the butter in a large, heavy-bottomed stockpot or Dutch oven over medium-high heat. Add the onions and cook, stirring every few minutes, until they begin to soften, about 5 minutes. Reduce the heat to medium and continue cooking, stirring every few minutes, until the onions are evenly browned and almost completely collapsed, about 15 more minutes. Add the garlic and cook, stirring, for 5 more minutes. Season with salt and pepper.

Add the port, cider, beef broth, thyme sprig, and apples. Bring to a gentle boil and cook for 5 minutes. Reduce heat and simmer for 1 hour.

To serve, preheat the broiler. For easy handling, place six oven-safe serving bowls on a rimmed baking sheet. Divide the soup between bowls, then top each with ⅓ cup croutons and ⅓ cup grated Gruyère. Broil until the cheese is melted, browned, and bubbling. Serve immediately.

3 cups whole milk

¼ cup chopped fresh tarragon

1 teaspoon salt

3 ripe avocados

Juice of ½ lemon

Pinch cayenne pepper

Freshly ground black pepper

Fresh tarragon leaves, for garnish

Serves 6 to 8

Avocado Bisque

9 TABLES FINE DINING, THE PLAINS ❧ CHEF WILLIAM JUSTICE

9 Tables is just that—a restaurant with only nine tables, and just one seating a night. The prix fixe menu offers an intimate, immersive dining experience. This cold, creamy soup appears on 9 Tables' summer menu and is enlivened with the licorice bite of fresh tarragon.

In a medium saucepan, combine the milk, tarragon, and salt. Bring to a simmer over medium heat, then immediately remove from heat and let stand for an hour. Transfer to a high-speed blender and puree until the tarragon is no longer visible.

Scoop out the flesh of the avocados and add to the blender along with the lemon juice and cayenne pepper. Blend until smooth, season with black pepper to taste, and chill overnight. Divide between small serving bowls and garnish with fresh tarragon leaves.

(see photograph on page 71)

1 pound leeks

2 pounds celery root, peeled
    and cut into 2-inch chunks

1 cup heavy cream

2 cups whole milk

4 tablespoons unsalted butter,
    diced

2 cups hot, freshly brewed coffee

Kosher salt

Serves 12 as a first course

Celery Root and Young Leek Cappuccino with Crispy Fried Leek Tops

THE CULINARY VEGETABLE INSTITUTE, MILAN
CHEF LIAISON JAMIE SIMPSON

This intriguing soup is rich, smooth, and foamy like a great cappuccino. But celery root and leeks with coffee? Trust us, it works. While you can indeed taste the coffee, it's neither distracting nor out of place. Serve small bowls as a dinner party starter when the weather gets chilly. The crispy leek topping adds contrasting texture to the smooth soup. This recipe also halves well.

Cut the green tops of the leeks from the white bottoms and set the white bottoms aside. Trim any brown spots from the green tops. Carefully julienne the green tops, making sure they are all the same width so they fry consistently. Submerge in a bowl of cold water, swish around, and lift out onto a clean kitchen towel. Pat dry thoroughly.

Line a plate with paper towels. Heat 2 inches of vegetable oil to 300 degrees in a large skillet or Dutch oven. Carefully add the dry, julienned leek tops and fry until they just stop bubbling. Remove with a slotted spoon and drain on the paper towels.

Roughly chop the reserved leek bottoms and set in a bowl of cool water to wash. In a small stockpot or large saucepan, combine the chopped leek bottoms, peeled celery root, cream, and milk. The vegetables should be submerged in the milk. If they're not, add more milk and cream. Bring to a simmer and cook gently over medium-low heat until the vegetables are tender, about 10 minutes.

Working in batches if necessary, process in a blender until very smooth. On low speed, add the diced butter one cube at a time. Adjust the consistency with coffee to taste (you may not need all 2 cups). Season to taste with salt, divide between bowls, garnish with fried leek tops, and serve.

Cheddar Beer Soup

MAUMEE BAY BREWING COMPANY, TOLEDO
CHEF STEVEN AUXTER

Maumee Bay Brewing Company's Buckeye Beer dates back to 1838. It's Toledo's hometown easy-drinking pilsner. At the brewery's pub, Buckeye Beer adds a backbone to this, their signature soup. If you can't get Buckeye, be sure to use a crisp lager or pilsner and not a hoppy ale, which would make the soup bitter.

3 tablespoons unsalted butter

¼ cup finely diced onion

¼ cup finely diced carrot

¼ cup finely diced celery

3 tablespoons all-purpose flour

1 cup low-sodium chicken stock

1 cup heavy cream

1 cup Buckeye Beer or other good-quality pilsner beer

½ teaspoon hot pepper sauce

5 ounces (1 generous cup) grated Cheddar cheese

5 ounces processed cheese loaf (such as Velveeta™), cut into ½-inch cubes (about 1 cup)

Salt and freshly ground black pepper

Serves 4

In a medium heavy-bottomed pot, melt the butter over medium heat. Add the onions, carrots, and celery and cook until soft, about 5 minutes. Whisk in the flour and cook, whisking constantly, until a golden paste forms, about 3 minutes. Raise the heat to medium-high and add the chicken stock, whisking until smooth.

Return to a boil, then add the cream and beer. Reduce the heat to medium-low and simmer for 10 minutes, whisking frequently so the bottom of the pot does not scorch. Add the hot pepper sauce and Cheddar and processed cheeses and stir until melted. Let simmer gently for 5 minutes, then season to taste with salt and pepper and serve.

❧ **Note:** *This is a very rich and filling soup, but if you are serving people with hearty appetites, you may want to double the recipe.*

Soup

4 chicken leg quarters
(about 5 pounds)

2 medium carrots, peeled and
cut into large chunks

2 medium celery stalks, cut into
large chunks

2 medium onions, cut into
large chunks

1 cup dry white wine

8 cups low-sodium chicken stock

Noodles

2 to 3 cups all-purpose flour

1 teaspoon baking soda

1 teaspoon baking powder

1 teaspoon salt

4 eggs, preferably local
and farm-raised

Salt and freshly ground
black pepper

Serves 8

Chicken and Noodles

THE HOUSE OF WINES, MARIETTA
CHEF-OWNER SALLY OLIVER

In her restaurant and wine and beer shop overlooking the Muskingum River, Chef Oliver serves new American cuisine. But for the annual Octoberfest, Oliver makes this filling home-style dish, beloved of many families in the Appalachian foothills of southeast Ohio. For fans, it's not a holiday meal without homemade noodles. The white wine in the broth is not traditional, but it lends a welcome complexity.

For the soup:

In a large Dutch oven or heavy-bottomed stockpot (at least a 6-quart capacity), combine the chicken, carrots, celery, onions, wine, and chicken stock. Bring to a boil, reduce to a simmer, cover, and cook until the chicken is tender, 30 to 45 minutes. Strain, reserving the broth. Pull the chicken meat from the bones and discard the vegetables and skin, but reserve the bones. Cool the meat, then refrigerate.

Meanwhile, return the broth and bones to the stockpot. Bring to a gentle simmer and cook for about 2 hours. Strain, then skim the fat from the surface. (The broth may be made up to 2 days in advance, cooled, and refrigerated. Scrape the solidified fat from the surface and discard.)

For the noodles:

In a large bowl, mix together 2 cups of the flour, baking soda, baking powder, and salt. Make a well in the center and crack the eggs into it. With a table knife, whisk the eggs while slowly incorporating the flour mixture. If needed, add more flour a bit at a time to make a dough that's soft but not sticky. Turn out the dough onto a clean surface dusted with flour and knead to form a smooth ball (wet your hands if necessary to keep the dough from sticking). Cover with plastic wrap and let rest for 30 to 60 minutes at room temperature.

On a lightly floured surface, roll out the dough ¼ inch thick. Using a sharp knife, cut noodles in ½-inch-wide strips. Toss cut noodles into a flat container dusted with flour. If not cooking the noodles immediately, cover with plastic wrap to keep fresh (cook the noodles within a few hours of making the dough, as they will eventually dry out, even if covered).

To assemble:

Bring the broth to a low simmer. Add the noodles and cook until they are fluffy and thick, at least 25 to 30 minutes (do not boil, or the noodles will be tough). Add the cooked chicken and cook until warmed through, about 5 minutes. Taste, adjust seasoning with salt and pepper if needed, and serve.

Italian Sausage, Kale, and Cannellini Bean Soup

FERRANTE WINERY, GENEVA ❧ CHEF NINA SALERNO

Ohio has a surprisingly long history of winemaking—in 1860, it led the nation in wine production. The southern shores of Lake Erie form the Grand River Valley American Viticultural Area, which boasts a unique climate. Ferrante Winery, founded in 1937, uses both American and European varietals, and is particularly well known for its white wines. Ferrante's plucky Gruner Veltliner gives this hearty-but-not-heavy soup a lift.

1 pound sweet Italian sausage (casings removed)

1 cup chopped carrots

1 cup chopped yellow onions

3 garlic cloves, chopped

½ cup Ferrante's Gruner Veltliner

6 cups low-sodium chicken stock

2 (14.5-ounce) cans diced tomatoes

1 (15-ounce) can great northern or cannellini beans, drained and rinsed

1 tablespoon dried basil

1 teaspoon salt

1 teaspoon freshly ground black pepper

8 ounces (about 4 loosely packed cups) fresh kale leaves, stemmed and roughly chopped

1 ounce (½ cup) grated Romano cheese, plus more for serving

Serves 6

In a large stockpot, cook the sausage over medium heat until browned, 5 to 7 minutes, breaking the sausage into small pieces as it cooks.

Add the carrots, onions, and garlic. Cook, stirring often, for 5 to 7 minutes. Add the wine and cook until the wine has reduced somewhat, 2 to 3 minutes.

Add the stock, tomatoes, beans, basil, salt, and pepper.

Bring the soup to a boil. Reduce the heat and simmer for 10 minutes. Add the kale and Romano cheese and cook for 3 minutes. Serve with additional grated Romano cheese, if desired.

❧ **Note:** *If Ferrante's Grand River Valley Gruner Veltliner is not available, use a good dry or off-dry white wine.*

Gazpacho

1 medium cucumber

2 to 3 Roma tomatoes

2 red bell peppers

Half a jalapeño pepper
(keep the seeds for more
heat or remove for less)

1 garlic clove

¼ cup diced red onion

½ cup lobster, fish, or shrimp stock

3 tablespoons red wine vinegar

½ cup extra-virgin olive oil

4 ounces cooked and chilled
lobster meat

1 ¼ cups V8® vegetable juice

Tabasco™ hot pepper sauce

Salt and freshly ground
black pepper

Lobster salad

4 ounces cooked lobster meat

¼ cup mayonnaise

1 tablespoon minced shallot

2 tablespoons thinly sliced
fresh chives

Salt and freshly ground
black pepper

Lobster Gazpacho

GRANVILLE INN, GRANVILLE & EXECUTIVE CHEF CHAD LAVELY

Gazpacho hits the spot on a balmy day. Adding sweet and cool chunks of lobster is an ingenious touch, and crunchy crostini with creamy lobster salad tops it all off. There couldn't be a more notable place to enjoy a cup than the stately grounds of the Granville Inn, which was built in 1924 and is now owned by nearby Denison University.

For the gazpacho:
Peel the cucumber, then halve and scrape out the seedy insides with a metal spoon. Reserve the seeds. Chop the flesh into ¼-inch dice. Halve and seed the tomatoes, reserving the seeds. Chop the flesh into ¼-inch dice. Core the red bell peppers; remove and discard the ribs. Chop into ¼-inch dice. You should have about 1 cup of each diced vegetable. Place in a large bowl and set aside.

In a blender, combine the reserved cucumber and tomato seeds with the jalapeño pepper and garlic. Puree until smooth and pour over the diced vegetables in the bowl. Add the onions, lobster stock, vinegar, and olive oil. Pull the lobster meat into small chunks with your hands and add to the bowl. Add enough V8® to make the mixture soupy but not thin (you may not need all the V8®). Season to taste with Tabasco™, salt, and pepper. Chill for 12 hours or overnight.

For the lobster salad:
Pull the lobster meat into small chunks with your hands and place in a medium bowl. Gently fold in the mayonnaise, shallots, and chives and season to taste with salt and pepper. Chill.

(continued on page 80)

Crostini

1 baguette

2 tablespoons extra-virgin olive oil

Salt and freshly ground
   black pepper

Serves 8 as an appetizer
   or 4 as an entrée

For the crostini:
Preheat the oven to 350 degrees.

Slice the baguette on a bias into slices ¼ inch thick and put them in a large bowl. Drizzle with the oil, then season with salt and pepper and toss to combine. Arrange the slices on a rimmed baking sheet (you may need more than one sheet). Bake until slices are hard in the center, 8 to 15 minutes. Let cool. (Crostini may be made up to a week in advance and kept in an airtight container.)

To serve:
Divide the gazpacho between serving bowls. For every portion, spoon a generous dollop of lobster salad onto a crostino and lay on top of the gazpacho. Serve immediately.

❧ **Note:** *If you boiled lobster tails in their shells for the meat, strain and chill the cooking liquid to use as lobster stock in the gazpacho.*

About 1 pound filet mignon
(two 6- to 8-ounce steaks)

1 pound ground beef
(80/20 is good)

1 (14½-ounce) can diced
tomatoes

1 (14½-ounce) can light red
kidney beans, including liquid

1 (8-ounce) can tomato sauce

1 small onion, minced

1 tablespoon air-dried red and
green bell peppers (optional)

1 (1¼-ounce) packet McCormick
chili seasoning (mild or hot)

1¼ teaspoons chili powder

½ teaspoon crushed red
pepper flakes

4 turns of freshly ground
black pepper

½ teaspoon salt

3 tablespoons brown sugar

4 to 8 small pickled jalapeño rings,
finely chopped, divided

1 tablespoon brine from the
jar of pickled jalapeños

2 tablespoons water

Serves 6

Melanie's Prizewinning Tenderloin Chili

MELANIE TIENTER, LITTLE HOCKING

This book's photographer has a secret past life as a frequent participant in chili cook-offs in Ohio and West Virginia. This is the recipe she's developed over the years. Her secret weapon? Meaty bits of grilled beef tenderloin that give it a great texture. It's on the spicy end of the spectrum, with a balanced sweet-tart finish. Melanie likes it with a peanut butter sandwich—a little-known regional accompaniment that's unexpectedly great. She also sometimes omits the beans and uses this as a hot dog sauce.

Season the steaks with salt and pepper. Grill over high heat until well marked, to about medium-well doneness. (If grilling isn't an option, sear the steaks in a hot skillet). Set aside to cool slightly.

In a large, heavy-bottomed pot or Dutch oven over medium heat, cook the ground beef until crumbly and no longer pink. Skim off most of the grease and juices and discard.

Add the diced tomatoes, beans, tomato sauce, onions, dried bell peppers, spices, pepper, and salt. Remove any gristle from the steaks and discard. Shred into bite-size pieces and add to the pot. Bring to a boil, and then add the brown sugar, half of the chopped jalapeño, and the jalapeño brine. Reduce to a simmer and gently cook for about 1 hour. Adjust the consistency with water, if needed, and then adjust seasoning with more salt, if needed. If you want the chili to be spicier, add as much of the remaining jalapeño as desired.

Soup

4 tablespoons unsalted butter

1 large onion, finely diced

1 teaspoon minced fresh ginger

1 large garlic clove, minced

2 tablespoons white wine

1 pound crimini mushrooms,
  cleaned and roughly chopped

2 cups water

¼ cup shiro miso

½ cup heavy cream

Freshly squeezed juice of ½ lime

1 teaspoon balsamic vinegar

¼ teaspoon cayenne pepper

Salt and freshly ground
  black pepper

Garnish

1 teaspoon balsamic vinegar

1 tablespoon thinly sliced
  fresh chives (optional)

Serves 4 to 8

Miso Mushroom Soup

TARRAGON AT THE INN AT HONEY RUN, MILLERSBURG
CHEF BRET ANDREASEN

This rich soup has a delicate miso flavor. Shiro miso is sometimes known as white miso or sweet miso, and can be found at most well-stocked grocery stores.

For the soup:
In a 4-quart saucepan or Dutch oven, melt the butter over medium-low heat. Add the onions and cook until translucent, about 5 minutes. Add the ginger and garlic and cook until fragrant, about 1 minute. Increase the heat to medium–high, add the white wine, and cook until almost dry.

Add the mushrooms and cook, stirring frequently, until they release enough of their own liquid that they are nearly covered. Add the water, bring to a boil, and reduce to a simmer. Cover and cook for 30 minutes.

Add the miso paste to the pot and puree the mixture until completely smooth (you may need to do this in batches if using a blender or food processor). Return the soup to the pan and add the heavy cream, lime juice, balsamic vinegar, and cayenne. Season with salt and pepper to taste.

To serve:
Divide between bowls. Garnish with tiny drops of balsamic vinegar and a small sprinkling of chives, if you like. Cooled and refrigerated, the soup will keep for 5 days.

½ cup (1 stick) unsalted butter

6 medium onions, thinly sliced

2 tablespoons sugar

Salt and freshly ground black pepper

4 cups low-sodium chicken stock

½ cup heavy cream

1 ounce (½ cup) grated
    Asiago cheese

1 ounce (½ cup) grated
    Parmesan cheese

1 ounce (½ cup) grated
    Romano cheese

Serves 8 to 10

Onion Bisque

MURPHIN RIDGE INN, WEST UNION
OWNER PAULA SCHUTT

This was voted "Best of the City" by Cincinnati Magazine. *It's cheesy and just a little bit sweet, and tender bits of long-cooked onions give it an appealing texture.*

Melt the butter in a Dutch oven or medium, heavy–bottomed stockpot over medium heat. Add the onions and cook, stirring occasionally, until they begin to soften. Sprinkle with the sugar and continue cooking until quite limp (do not brown). Season with salt and pepper. Add the chicken stock, bring to a boil, reduce to a simmer, and cook for 45 minutes.

Blend the soup in batches in a food processor, or in the stockpot with an immersion blender. The soup should still be chunky, but with no long strands of onion. Return the soup to the pot. Add the cream and cheeses and heat the soup through slowly, stirring until the cheeses are melted. Season to taste with salt and pepper and serve.

Roasted chestnut soup

3 to 3½ cups (1 pound) chestnuts

3 tablespoons plus ½ cup (1 stick) unsalted butter, cold, divided

½ cup chopped onion

4 garlic cloves, crushed

1 cup dry white wine

5 to 6 cups low-sodium chicken stock (or homemade)

Sprigs from ½ bunch fresh thyme

2 bay leaves

2 tablespoons Worcestershire sauce

Salt and freshly ground black pepper

Brandy crèma

¼ cup heavy cream

1½ tablespoons brandy, cognac, or sherry

Pinch salt and freshly ground black pepper

Serves 6

Oven-Roasted Chestnut Soup with Brandy Crèma

REGISTRY BISTRO, TOLEDO CHEF ERICA RAPP

This delightful soup does a nifty trick at the table as the crèma rises to the surface and creates a frothy pattern. The texture is exceptionally silky from pureed chestnuts and a generous hand with the butter, while the touch of brandy in the crèma cuts through the richness. Despite the cream and chestnuts, make no mistake: this is a savory soup, one that's perfect for serving at the beginning of a fall or winter meal.

For the roasted chestnut soup:
To roast the chestnuts, preheat the oven to 350 degrees. Score an X in the shells of the chestnuts with a sharp paring knife. Spread on a rimmed baking sheet and roast the chestnuts for 35 minutes. While they are still hot, remove and discard the outer skin. Set aside.

Melt 3 tablespoons of the butter in a large, heavy-bottomed saucepan or Dutch oven over medium-low heat. Stir in the onions and garlic and sweat until translucent. Increase the heat to medium-high, add the wine, bring to a boil, and cook until reduced by three-quarters.

Add 5 cups of the chicken stock, thyme sprigs, bay leaves, and the roasted chestnuts. Reduce the heat and simmer, uncovered, until chestnuts are soft, about 1 hour.

Remove the thyme and bay leaves, then puree the soup until smooth (if using a blender, you may need to do this in batches). Adjust the consistency with more chicken stock, if needed; the soup should have a nice body, but not be gloppy.

Return the pureed soup to the pot and add the Worcestershire sauce. Cut the remaining stick of cold butter into cubes and whisk it into the soup, a few cubes at a time. Season to taste with salt and pepper. Keep the soup warm over low heat while you make the brandy crèma.

For the brandy crèma:
Whip the cream to soft peaks, then add the brandy, cognac, or sherry. Season with salt and pepper to taste.

To serve:
Put a dollop of the savory crèma in the bottom of each bowl, fill with soup, then add more crèma over the hot soup. The cream will rise to the top and resemble crèma in a cappuccino. Serve immediately.

❦ **Note:** *If fresh chestnuts are unavailable, substitute a 14.8-ounce jar of cooked chestnuts (3 cups peeled chestnuts) and skip the roasting step.*

2 tablespoons olive oil

1 large onion, diced

3 garlic cloves, minced

2 tablespoons tomato paste

½ teaspoon cumin

½ teaspoon curry powder

¼ teaspoon freshly ground
     black pepper

1 cup red lentils

1 bay leaf

5 cups low-sodium chicken stock

Salt

Serves 4

Red Lentil Soup (Shorbat Adas)

THE BUCKLEY HOUSE, MARIETTA ❧ CHEF EMAD AL-MASRI

The Buckley House serves Mediterranean-influenced Continental fare in an elegantly decorated Victorian house just steps away from the heart of historical downtown Marietta. Al-Masri also offers dishes reflecting his heritage, including this satisfying and flavorful soup. At The Buckley House, you can enjoy it with their irresistible freshly baked pita, as well as turnips pickled in a brine tinged pink from beet juice.

Heat the olive oil in a large Dutch oven or heavy-bottomed stockpot over medium-high heat. Add the onions and cook, stirring occasionally, until translucent, 6 minutes. Add the garlic and cook for 1 minute. Add the tomato paste and cook briefly, scraping the pan with a wooden spoon.

Add the spices, lentils, bay leaf, and stock and bring to a boil over high heat. Reduce to a simmer and cook, stirring occasionally so the lentils don't stick to the bottom of the pot and scorch. Simmer for about 30 minutes, until the lentils are tender and some are falling apart. The soup will thicken a little as it cools. Taste and season with salt as needed, and serve immediately.

Cooled, covered, and refrigerated, the soup will keep for several days.

Main
Courses

Asiago Chicken Burgers, p. 88

2 ounces (½ cup) coarsely grated
    Asiago cheese

¼ cup finely chopped sun-dried
    tomatoes (oil-packed or supple
    and soft like raisins)

¼ cup fresh baby spinach, chopped

½ teaspoon freshly ground
    white pepper

1 teaspoon salt

½ teaspoon garlic powder
    or 1 fresh garlic clove, minced

2 pounds ground chicken
    breast meat

Serves 6

Asiago Chicken Burgers

GRAMMA DEBBIE'S KITCHEN AT FINDLAY MARKET, CINCINNATI
CHEF-OWNER DEBBIE KNUEVEN GANNAWAY

Cincinnati's bustling Findlay Market is Ohio's oldest continuously open public market. It hosts an outdoor farmers market seasonally, while in the indoor portion, dozens of vendors sell foods and wares. Gramma Debbie's Kitchen is a popular spot for prepared foods. These flavorful chicken burgers are a perennial favorite with customers, who often get a pan of baked beans, potato salad, or pre-sliced burger fixings while they're at it.

In a medium bowl, combine cheese, sun-dried tomatoes, spinach, and seasonings; toss to combine. In a large bowl, combine the ground chicken with the vegetable-spice mixture. Knead together thoroughly with your hands, then form into six patties.

To cook, grill over medium-high heat for 8 to 10 minutes, until the internal temperature registers 165 degrees on an instant-read thermometer. (You may also cook the burgers in a skillet filmed with vegetable oil over medium-high heat.) Serve the cooked patties on buns with lettuce, tomatoes, onions, and mayonnaise on the side.

☙ **Note:** *Good-quality ground chicken is imperative to the success of this recipe. Pre-packed ground chicken will cook up mealy and dry. See if your favorite meat counter can grind chicken breasts for you, or grind your own: use boneless, skinless chicken breasts, and don't trim off the fat.*

(see photograph on page 87)

Fondue

12 ounces (3 cups) grated
   Guggisberg Baby Swiss cheese

6 ounces (1½ cups) grated
   Gruyère cheese

1 tablespoon cornstarch

⅛ teaspoon minced garlic

¾ cup dry white wine

2 tablespoons dry sherry

Accompaniments

Cubed crusty French bread

Sliced cooked bratwurst

Boiled skin-on baby potatoes

Blanched broccoli pieces

Sliced fresh pear

Serves 4

Baby Swiss Cheese Fondue

CHALET IN THE VALLEY, MILLERSBURG
CHEF JEFF ALLISON

Founded by Swiss émigré Alfred Guggisberg at the request of Amish farmers who wanted an expert cheesemaker to use their milk, Guggisberg Cheese makes the original Baby Swiss. Alfred developed a creamy, mild style of Swiss cheese to suit American palates, and it continues to garner industry awards today. Visitors can stop in the Guggisberg factory in Millersburg to see it made—with its elaborate chalet-style façade, it beckons Amish Country tourists and cheese lovers year-round. Guggisberg Baby Swiss is the key ingredient in this fondue, perhaps the best cheese fondue we've ever tasted.

In a gallon zip-top bag, toss the grated cheeses with the cornstarch until evenly coated. Set aside.

In a fondue pot or medium nonreactive saucepan over medium heat, add the garlic and cook quickly for 10 seconds (do not brown). Immediately add the white wine and bring to a boil.

Add the Baby Swiss and Gruyère cheeses a handful at a time, stirring constantly. When the cheese is melted and smooth, stir in the dry sherry. If the fondue is too thick, add more wine; if it is too thin, add more cheese.

Transfer to a fondue pot over a burner (if using). Adjust the flame so the fondue bubbles gently. If the flame is too low, the fondue will separate, but don't panic—it will come right back together with more heat and lots of stirring. Serve with desired accompaniments.

Beef Neck Roast
Braised in Red Wine

CROSSWINDS GRILLE AT THE LAKEHOUSE INN, GENEVA
CHEF NATE FAGNILLI

"This, in my opinion, is the king of all pot roasts," says Chef Fagnilli, who should know. Not only is he the chef at Crosswinds Grille, he also runs Na*Kyrsie Meats, doing whole-animal butchery. "Cattle are grazers with big heads," he says, "so the neck muscles do a lot of work." Those burly muscles become meltingly tender after hours of braising in stock and red wine, turning mere pot roast into a revelation. Like all braises, it's best when made a day ahead.

1 (5-pound) bone-in neck roast,
    or brisket, chuck, or other
    braising cut

Salt and freshly ground
    black pepper

1 to 2 tablespoons vegetable oil

1 white onion, cut into 1-inch chunks

2 carrots, peeled and cut
    into 1-inch chunks

2 celery ribs, cut into 1-inch chunks

3 garlic cloves, smashed

1 sprig rosemary

2 sprigs thyme

1 bay leaf

2 cups dry red wine

4 cups low-sodium beef stock

Serves 6 to 8

Season the roast generously with salt and pepper a day or two before cooking and refrigerate, uncovered.

Preheat the oven to 350 degrees.

Heat the oil in a large Dutch oven on medium heat. Add the roast and brown well on all sides.

Remove and let rest on a sheet pan. Add the vegetables to the pot and cook until softened, 6 to 8 minutes. Add the garlic and herbs, then the red wine. Simmer until reduced by half.

Return the roast to the pot and add enough stock to come halfway up the roast (you may not need all 4 cups). Cover, place in the oven, and cook until a fork slides into the meat easily and the meat is falling off the bone. Start checking after 2 hours; the total time will depend on the size, shape, and type of cut (plan on up to 8 hours, though it may take just 3 or 4). Cool, then cover and refrigerate overnight.

Remove and discard any solidified fat. Strain the liquid; discard the vegetables and herbs. Pull the meat from the bone and slice across the grain into serving pieces. Warm in the strained braising liquid. Season the liquid with salt and pepper to taste and serve with the meat.

✺ **Note:** *If you like, add cubed potatoes to the pot for the last 1 to 1½ hours of cooking and serve as a side.*

2 cups water

1 cup long-grain white rice
(not converted)

1 large head cabbage, cored

3 pounds ground beef
(80/20 is good)

1 tablespoon dry onion soup mix

1 teaspoon Cajun seasoning

1 ½ teaspoons salt

2 ¼ teaspoons dried dill

2 (15-ounce) cans tomato sauce,
divided

1 pound fresh sauerkraut,
not drained

2 tablespoons brown sugar

6 slices bacon

Makes 10 large rolls,
enough to serve 6

Cabbage Rolls

RIP'S CAFÉ, STRUTHERS   ❧   CHEF-OWNER MARILYN WATT

Chef-owner Marilyn Watt has worked at Rip's Café all her adult life. Established in 1933, Rip's is a neighborhood joint known for Hungarian food. At Rip's, they call cabbage rolls "pigs," short for "pigs in a blanket." Make a giant batch; these rolls freeze beautifully in their sweet and tangy sauce. Serve them with mashed potatoes to sop up all the sauce.

Bring the 2 cups water to boil. Add the rice, cover, and remove from heat. Set aside and let rest for 30 minutes.

Place the cabbage in a microwave-safe bowl. Add 4 inches of water and microwave on high, uncovered, for 13 minutes. The cabbage will be pliable and not fully cooked. Set aside to cool.

In a large bowl, combine the ground beef, soup mix, Cajun seasoning, salt, and dill. Drain the rice (discard the soaking water). Add the rice to the beef mixture and work with your hands until thoroughly combined.

Preheat the oven to 450 degrees with a rack in the center of the oven.

Carefully separate the cabbage leaves so they do not tear. Make a stack of the biggest leaves (you want about a dozen) and save a few of the smaller ones for patching. Ultimately, you won't use all the cabbage.

Lay a cabbage leaf on a clean work surface. With your hands, form ⅔ cup of the filling into an oblong shape. Set in the center of a leaf and roll up to create a package. Place in a deep 9 x 13-inch baking pan or 2½-quart casserole, seam side down. You should have about ten rolls; you may have to pack them in tightly.

(continued on page 92)

Top with one can of the tomato sauce, then add the sauerkraut, sprinkle with the brown sugar, and layer the bacon evenly over the rolls. Top with the remaining can of sauce. Add water to just come level with the rolls, if necessary.

Cover the pan with foil and cook for 1½ hours. Reduce the heat to 250 degrees and cook another 1 to 2 hours, until the cabbage is very tender and the juices are boiling rapidly. Let sit for 10 minutes before serving, with the sauce on the side.

∞ *Note:* *Any unused onion soup mix can be saved for future use, or simply mixed with sour cream for chip dip. Why not?*

Meatloaf

Nonstick cooking spray

1 tablespoon olive oil, divided

¼ cup finely diced onion

2 cups (3½ ounces) sliced
   shiitake mushrooms

1 pound ground beef

4 ounces ground veal

10 ounces ground pork

1 large egg

¾ cup dried bread crumbs

1½ teaspoons finely chopped
   fresh parsley

½ teaspoon finely chopped
   fresh thyme

½ teaspoon finely chopped
   fresh sage

1 tablespoon roasted garlic,
   mashed into a paste (see Note)

1 tablespoon heavy cream

¾ teaspoon Worcestershire sauce

1 teaspoon salt

½ teaspoon finely ground
   black pepper

2 tablespoons barbecue sauce

Cap City Fine Diner Meatloaf with Barbecue Gravy

CAP CITY FINE DINER, GRANDVIEW AND GAHANNA
REGIONAL CHEF PETER CHAPMAN

The beloved atmosphere of American diners gets an upscale spin at Cap City Fine Diner, where chrome and Formica meet shallots and shiitakes. This meatloaf, a longtime customer favorite, follows suit. Cap City Fine Diner serves it on a thick slab of bread and tops it with mashed potatoes, barbecue gravy, and Chili Onion Rings (see page 50 in Salads & Sides). But don't worry—it's easily good enough to stand alone.

For the meatloaf:
Preheat the oven to 325 degrees. Spray a 6 x 9 x 4-inch loaf pan with nonstick cooking spray.

In a small skillet, heat ½ tablespoon of the olive oil over medium-high heat. Add the onions and cook until lightly browned, about 5 minutes. Remove to a small bowl, return the skillet to the heat, add the remaining ½ tablespoon oil, and
cook the mushrooms until they are softened but not mushy, about 5 minutes. Add to the bowl with the onions; set aside to cool.

Meanwhile, in the bowl of an electric mixer, add the ground beef, veal, and pork, then the egg, bread crumbs, herbs, garlic, and cream. Mix well on low speed with the paddle attachment (or use your hands). Add the Worcestershire sauce, salt, pepper, and the cooked mushrooms and onions. Continue mixing on low speed until combined.

Pack the mixture into the prepared loaf pan. Set the loaf pan in a large pan at least 4 inches deep (a roasting pan works well). Fill the large pan with enough hot tap water to come halfway up the sides of the loaf pan. Tightly cover the large pan with foil and bake for 90 minutes.

(continued on page 94)

Barbecue gravy

2 tablespoons unsalted butter

2 tablespoons chopped onion

1 garlic clove, chopped

¼ cup all-purpose flour

1 cup low-sodium beef broth

1 cup bottled barbecue sauce

Salt and freshly ground
    black pepper

Serves 8

Remove the foil, spread the barbecue sauce over the meatloaf, and continue baking until an instant–read thermometer inserted in the center of the meatloaf registers 155 degrees, about 15 to 30 minutes. Remove the roasting pan from the oven and allow the meatloaf to rest in the water bath for 10 minutes before slicing and serving.

For the barbecue gravy:
In a medium saucepan, melt the butter over medium heat. Add the onions and cook until soft, about 4 minutes. Add the garlic and cook for 1 minute. Beat in the flour to make a smooth paste. Slowly whisk in the beef broth, followed by the barbecue sauce. Simmer for 15 minutes, whisking occasionally. Strain, taste, and adjust seasoning with salt and pepper, if needed. Serve over the meatloaf.

To serve:
For the full diner experience, follow Cap City's lead. Place half a hamburger bun on a plate, lay on a thick slice of meatloaf, and drizzle with barbecue gravy. Add a dollop of mashed potatoes and top with Chili Onion Rings *(see page 50 in Sides & Salads)*.

❧ **Note:** *To roast garlic, preheat the oven to 400 degrees. Cut the tops off one or more heads of garlic and rub a little olive oil on the cut surfaces. Wrap the garlic loosely in foil and roast until golden brown and soft, 40 to 60 minutes.*

Chili

2 (6-ounce) cans tomato paste

2 onions, finely diced

6 garlic cloves, peeled and minced

2 tablespoons chili powder

1 teaspoon ground cumin

½ teaspoon cayenne pepper

1 teaspoon cinnamon

¾ teaspoon allspice

¼ teaspoon cloves

1 bay leaf

2 tablespoons unsweetened
cocoa powder

5 cups water

2 pounds lean ground beef
(4 percent fat)

2 tablespoons apple cider
or white vinegar

1 tablespoon Worcestershire sauce

2 teaspoons kosher salt

Options for serving

Oyster crackers

Hot cooked spaghetti

Finely shredded Cheddar cheese

1 can kidney or pinto beans,
drained and heated

½ onion, finely chopped

Serves 6 to 8

Cincinnati Chili

SARA BIR, THE SAUSAGETARIAN

Of all the chili styles in the United States, the Queen City's might be the most storied. Thick and unusually spiced, Cincinnati chili—created by bothers John and Tom Kiradjieff in 1922 at Empress Chili—occupies its own galaxy in the chili universe. It sauces hot dogs and goes solo in steaming bowls. Most commonly, it tops cooked spaghetti (think of it as Cincinnati Bolognese). It's also incredibly easy to make, since the authentic method is to dump everything in the pot at once and let it simmer. While not light fare by any means, its wholesomeness may surprise you when you make it at home with good ingredients.

For the chili:
Heat a large, heavy-bottomed pot over medium-high heat and add the tomato paste. Cook about a minute or two, scraping the bottom of the pot constantly to keep the paste from burning but letting it brown slightly. Add the remaining ingredients and stir vigorously to break up the meat.

Bring to a boil, reduce to a simmer, and cook, stirring frequently, until the chili is thick and pasty, about 2½ hours. Taste and adjust seasoning, if necessary.

For serving:
Serve with the garnishes and accompaniments of your choice.

For a two-way: Serve the chili on spaghetti.

For a three-way: Serve the chili on spaghetti with grated Cheddar cheese.

For a four-way: Serve the chili on spaghetti with grated Cheddar cheese and chopped onions.

For a five-way: Serve the chili on spaghetti with grated Cheddar cheese, chopped onions, and beans.

4 red bell peppers

1 ¼ cups low-sodium vegetable stock

1 cup couscous

1 tablespoon olive oil

¼ cup sliced shallot

¼ cup minced garlic

1 cup thinly sliced mushrooms

⅓ cup pine nuts

1 cup chopped fresh spinach
or arugula

1 tablespoon za'atar, plus more
for sprinkling

½ cup crumbled feta cheese

Salt

4 (¼-inch) slices feta cheese

Serves 4

Couscous-Stuffed Peppers with Feta and Za'atar

NORTH MARKET SPICES, COLUMBUS
CO-OWNER BEN WALTERS

You can travel around the world in one visit to North Market Spices, at Columbus' North Market. The shop is packed with colorful spices and seasonings, enticing shoppers to discover new flavors and aromas. Walters uses the Middle Eastern blend za'atar in these gorgeous stuffed peppers. Za'atar's mixture of crushed sumac berries, dried herbs, and sesame seeds offsets the creamy and salty feta cheese of the couscous filling.

Preheat the oven to 350 degrees.

Cut the tops off the peppers and remove the cores and membranes. Place in a baking dish and bake, uncovered, until the skins are a little wrinkly, 30 to 40 minutes.

Bring the stock to a boil in a medium saucepan. Add the couscous, cover, and set aside to steam for 10 minutes.

Meanwhile, heat a medium skillet over medium–high heat. Add the oil; when it shimmers, add the shallots, garlic, and mushrooms and cook, stirring constantly, until the mushrooms shrivel and the shallots soften, about 3 minutes. Add the pine nuts and cook 1 minute more.

Fluff the couscous with a fork, then transfer to a large, heat–safe bowl. Scrape the cooked shallot mixture over the couscous, then add the spinach or arugula, za'atar, and crumbled feta. Mix thoroughly. Season to taste with salt or more za'atar, if needed.

Divide the filling between the peppers (do not overfill, or it will be dense) in the baking dish. Top each pepper with a slice of feta and sprinkle with za'atar. Bake until the feta and za'atar are lightly toasted, about 10 minutes.

❧ **Note:** *Some feta cheeses are saltier than others. Nibble the cheese before seasoning the couscous mixture—you may not need to add any salt.*

Filling

2 pounds pork shoulder

Salt and freshly ground
    black pepper

¼ cup dried cranberries

2 dried ancho chiles

1 dried guajillo chile

1 tablespoon olive oil

1 small onion, thinly sliced

½ teaspoon sea salt

⅓ cup unsweetened cranberry juice

½ cups fresh cranberries,
    washed and sorted

⅓ cup sugar

2 tablespoons maple syrup

½ teaspoon ground cumin

½ teaspoon ground coriander

⅛ teaspoon ground allspice

Dough and assembly

5 ounces dried corn husks

3½ cups masa harina

2 teaspoons kosher salt

2 to 3 cups low-sodium chicken
    or vegetable stock

1¼ cups good-quality lard
    or vegetable shortening,
    slightly softened

1½ teaspoons baking powder

Makes about 30 tamales

Cranberry Ancho Pork Tamales

NIXTAMALIZED, ATHENS
CHEF-OWNER MICHELLE WASSERMAN

A roving tamale cart, Nixtamalized uses fresh masa harina made from Shagbark Seed & Mill corn. Here we offer a recipe using easier-to-find masa harina (dry masa flour) instead. The tart cranberries offset the earthiness of the ancho chiles in the filling.

To braise the pork shoulder:

Season the pork shoulder with salt and pepper, place in a Dutch oven fat side up, and add enough water just to cover. Bring to a boil, reduce to just below a simmer, cover, and cook for 2 to 4 hours, turning the meat every 30 minutes or so. When the pork is fall-apart tender, remove from the pan, cool slightly, and pull into fine shreds.

To make the sauce:

Put the dried cranberries and chiles in a medium heat-safe bowl. Add enough boiling water to cover, making sure everything is immersed (weigh down with a small plate, if necessary). Steep for 15 minutes. Take the chiles out of the water and remove and discard the stems and seeds. Remove the cranberries. Strain and reserve the steeping water.

Heat the olive oil over medium heat in a medium saucepan. Add the onions and cook, stirring often, until translucent. Add the salt, reduce the heat to medium-low, and continue cooking until the onions are golden brown, about 10 minutes. Add the cranberry juice, ½ cup of the steeping water, the fresh cranberries, sugar, and maple syrup and bring to a boil. Add the spices and hydrated chiles and cranberries. Reduce to a simmer and cook for 20 minutes.

Blend with an immersion blender until smooth, then simmer 20 minutes more. The sauce should be thick but not too stiff; adjust the consistency with a little more reserved chile water, if needed. Add the shredded meat to the sauce and mix well. Taste for seasoning and add more salt, if needed. Cool slightly.

To make the dough, assemble, and steam the tamales:

Put the dried corn husks in a large pot or bowl. Fill the pot with

hot tap water, weigh down the husks with a plate, and soak for 15 minutes. Drain, then separate the corn husks, discarding any corn silk. Look for about thirty of the largest corn husks and put them on the top of the pile. Return all the husks to the pot or bowl, cover again with hot water, and soak for 30 minutes.

In a large bowl, whisk together the masa harina and salt. Stir in 2 cups of the stock and mix with your hands until the masa is no longer dry and holds together when squeezed. Add more stock, if necessary, to achieve the proper consistency.

With an electric mixer on medium–high speed, beat the lard or short-ening with the baking powder until creamy, about 1 minute. With the mixer on medium–low, add golf-ball–sized balls of masa. When all the masa is added, raise the speed to high and beat until light and fluffy, about 10 minutes. The dough should hold its shape in a spoon, but if it resembles Play-Doh, it's too stiff—add a little more stock.

Set a collapsible steamer rack in the bottom of a stockpot. Line the rack with torn or small corn husks (save the big ones for wrapping the tamales). Add water just to reach the bottom of the steamer.

Pat the separated husks dry with a towel. Lay one flat with the tapered end toward you. Spread about ¼ cup of the dough down the center, leaving at least a 1½-inch border along the sides. Spoon about 1½ tablespoons of the filling down the center of the dough. Pick up the long sides of the husk and bring them together, then fold over to one side. Finally, fold up the tapered end of the husk, leaving the top open. Repeat to fill thirty husks.

As they're made, stand the tamales on their folded bottoms in the pre-pared steamer. Pack them loosely so they have room to expand. (You may need to steam the tamales in two batches.)

When all the tamales are in the steamer, cover them with a layer of leftover cornhusks. Set the lid in place and steam over a constant medium heat for about 1¼ hours. The tamales are done when the husk peels away from the masa easily. Watch carefully that the water doesn't boil away; add boiling water to the pot as needed. Turn off the heat and let the tamales stand in the steamer off the heat for 10 minutes. To reheat leftovers, steam for 15 minutes.

2 cups all-purpose flour, divided

1 (12-ounce) bottle Dortmunder
Gold Lager

3 large eggs

1 cup cold water

1 teaspoon salt, plus more
for seasoning fish

1 cup cornstarch

2 pounds filleted whitefish
(walleye, cod, or tilapia)

Freshly ground black pepper

Vegetable oil, for frying

Lemon wedges, for serving

Serves 4

Dortmunder Gold Beer-Battered Fish

GREAT LAKES BREWING COMPANY, CLEVELAND

Great Lakes Brewing's balanced flagship lager has just the right character to make a crispy beer batter flavorful but not overpowering. Drink some while you fry the fish.

Place ½ cup of the flour in a shallow bowl or deep dinner plate. Set aside.

In a large bowl, whisk together the beer, eggs, water, and 1 teaspoon of the salt. Whisk in the cornstarch, then gradually whisk in the remaining 1½ cups flour.

If the fillets are large, cut them in half. Pat dry with paper towels and season with salt and pepper.

Line a tray with paper towels. Pour enough oil in a large cast-iron skillet or Dutch oven to create a depth of about 3 inches. Heat the oil to 350 degrees.

To fry, dredge a fish fillet in the flour. Dip the floured fillet in the batter and let the excess drip back into the bowl. Lower the fillet into the oil and fry until golden brown, 3 to 5 minutes, flipping halfway through. Drain briefly on the paper towels. Repeat with remaining fillets, adjusting the heat as needed so the oil stays between 350 and 375 degrees. Serve immediately, with lemon wedges on the side.

3 dried bay leaves

4 tablespoons apple cider vinegar,
   balsamic vinegar, or a
   combination of the two

5 garlic cloves, smashed
   and peeled

1 cup finely diced ripe
   and juicy tomatoes

12 peppercorns

3 to 4 tablespoons soy sauce

2 pounds bone-in, skin-on
   chicken thighs

1 tablespoon vegetable oil

1 to 2 tablespoons brown
   sugar (optional)

Serves 2 to 3

Filipino Chicken Adobo

THE INN AT DRESDEN, DRESDEN
INNKEEPER JOY ROTHENBERG

There are as many versions of chicken adobo as there are Filipino cooks, but the essence of the dish—chicken stewed with lots of vinegar, garlic, and peppercorns—remains constant. Dresden Inn owner Joy Rothenberg, who is from the Philippines, has adapted her chicken adobo to suit the tastes of her guests. The addition of tomatoes to the sauce brings a sweetness and depth, as does the option of using balsamic vinegar. Rothenberg serves it with mashed potatoes, but white rice is traditional. Either way, something starchy to soak up the glorious sauce is absolutely necessary.

Combine the bay leaves, vinegar, garlic, tomatoes, peppercorns, and 3 tablespoons of the soy sauce in a large (10-inch) skillet. Set the chicken on top, skin side down, and bring to a boil over medium-high heat. Reduce to a simmer and cook, turning the chicken over occasionally, until the chicken is tender and the tomatoes have completely broken down, about 30 minutes. Do not let the sauce boil dry; you may need to add a tablespoon or two of water to the skillet from time to time.

Remove the chicken and sauce from the pan. Wipe out the skillet, return to medium-high heat, and add the oil. Add back the chicken thighs, skin side down, and cook until browned, 1 to 2 minutes. Pour the sauce back into the pan. Taste and add more soy sauce, plus the sugar, if needed (depending on the sweetness of the tomatoes or vinegar you used, you may not need to add any sugar at all). The sauce should be salty, lightly sweet, and quite tart yet balanced. Serve immediately, with the sauce spooned on top. Leftovers will keep, refrigerated, for 5 days (chicken adobo is especially delicious the next day).

Meatloaf

1 cup fresh bread crumbs

1½ teaspoons garlic powder

1½ teaspoons onion powder

1½ teaspoons dried thyme

1 teaspoon freshly ground
    black pepper

1½ teaspoons salt

2 tablespoons heavy cream

2 large eggs, lightly beaten

1 pound ground pork

1 pound ground beef

Pastry

1½ cups all-purpose flour

¼ teaspoon salt

6 tablespoons unsalted butter,
    cold, cut into small cubes

2 large egg yolks

2 to 3 tablespoons heavy cream

To assemble

3 large egg yolks

1 tablespoon heavy cream

Serves 6 to 8

Hackbratentorte (German Crusted Meatloaf)

CANAL TAVERN OF ZOAR, BOLIVAR
EXECUTIVE CHEF CAMERON KRAHEL

Now a living-history museum, the hamlet of Zoar was settled in 1819 by Zoarites, immigrants from southwest Germany. The Canal Tavern building has housed restaurants since 1829. Today it dishes up German-influenced cuisine, such as this pâté-like meatloaf wrapped in a tender pastry crust. The tavern serves this with potato pancakes and dark brown gravy, but slices of leftovers are fantastic with nothing more than grainy mustard.

For the meatloaf:
Preheat the oven to 350 degrees with a rack in the center of the oven. Grease a 9 x 5-inch loaf pan.

In a large bowl, combine the bread crumbs, garlic powder, onion powder, thyme, pepper, and salt. Add the cream and eggs and stir to combine. Add the pork and beef and work with your hands until thoroughly combined (or blend in an electric mixer using the paddle attachment on low speed). The mixture will be very sticky. Pack it into the prepared pan, being careful to avoid forming air pockets. Level the top and cover with parchment paper, then foil. Bake until an instant-read thermometer inserted in the center of the meatloaf registers 160 degrees, 1 to 1½ hours. Cool on a wire rack until barely warm (*see Note*).

For the pastry:
Combine the flour and salt in the bowl of a food processor fitted with a steel blade. Scatter the cubed butter on top and pulse until the mixture resembles coarse sand.

(continued on page 104)

In a glass measuring cup, combine the egg yolks and 2 tablespoons cream. With the motor running, pour the mixture in a thin stream though the feed tube. Turn off the food processor and grab a wad of dough; it should form a cohesive blob when you squeeze it together. If it seems dry, add more cream, 1 tablespoon at a time.

Turn the dough onto a large sheet of plastic wrap and knead a few times to help it come together. Form it into a rough rectangle, wrap in the plastic, and chill for 30 minutes.

For the assembly and final baking:
Preheat the oven to 350 degrees. Line a rimmed baking sheet with foil.

Stir together 3 egg yolks and 1 tablespoon cream in a small bowl. Remove the baked and cooled meatloaf from its pan.

On a lightly floured surface, roll the chilled dough into a 13 x 10-inch rectangle. Brush all over with the egg yolk and cream mixture, then place the meatloaf upside down in the center. Fold the dough so it overlaps a bit on the bottom and sides, pressing down to make sure there are no gaps between the dough and the loaf. Trim off excess and, if necessary, use to patch up any holes.

Set the loaf seam side down on the prepared baking sheet. Brush all over with the egg yolk mixture. If you like, roll out dough scraps and cut out decorative leaf shapes. Place on the loaf and brush with the egg yolk mixture one more time.

Bake until the crust is shiny and golden brown and an instant-read thermometer inserted in the center of the meatloaf registers 150 degrees, 45 to 60 minutes. If needed, tent loosely with foil midway through baking to keep the crust from getting too dark. Cool on a wire rack for 10 minutes before slicing and serving.

  ∞ *Note: Be sure to let the meatloaf cool until barely warm before wrapping it in the pastry, or the heat will melt the butter and make the pastry unworkable.*

Pecan sauce

4 tablespoons unsalted butter

½ cup plus 2 tablespoons honey

½ cup pecan pieces

Chicken

4 boneless, skinless chicken
  breast halves

Salt and freshly ground
  black pepper

1 cup all-purpose flour

2 eggs

2 cups seasoned bread crumbs

2 cups olive oil

Serves 4

Honey Pecan Chicken

CREEKSIDE RESTAURANT & BAR, BRECKSVILLE
CHEF RICH WIDLICKA

Guests at Creekside Restaurant sit overlooking Chippewa Creek as it flows to nearby Cuyahoga Valley National Park. These chicken cutlets are one of their most popular dishes, and are served with roasted garlic mashed potatoes.

For the pecan sauce:
In a small saucepan, melt the butter over low heat. Add the honey and pecans. Keep warm over the lowest heat possible.

For the chicken:
With a meat pounder or rolling pin, pound the chicken breasts to an even thinness. Season with salt and pepper.

Put the flour in a wide, shallow bowl. Beat the eggs in another shallow bowl. Put the bread crumbs in a third bowl. Dredge a chicken breast in the flour, then dip in the eggs, and then in the bread crumbs to coat evenly. Place the breaded chicken on a parchment–lined tray; repeat with the remaining breasts.

Heat the oil to 325 degrees in a large, heavy–bottomed skillet with high sides. Add the chicken and fry until the breading is golden brown and an instant–read thermometer inserted in the chicken registers 165 degrees, about 3 to 5 minutes per side. (You'll probably need to fry the chicken in two batches.) Drain on paper towels, divide between plates, top with the pecan sauce, and serve immediately.

Hungarian Chicken Paprikás

THE AMBER ROSE, DAYTON
CHEFS LUKE HENRY AND T.J. PETERSON

Ohio has the largest population of Hungarian Americans in the country, and that heritage is reflected on the menus of restaurants in communities such as Akron and Dayton. For this traditional dish, make an effort to find good, fresh Hungarian paprika (hot or sweet)—look for a red tin in the spice aisle of most any grocery store. It'll make a significant difference in the flavor of the final dish. The Amber Rose serves this over spätzle, but egg noodles are also a fine accompaniment.

4 pounds boneless, skinless chicken thighs

Salt and freshly ground black pepper

1 cup water

1½ teaspoons vegetable oil

1 medium onion, chopped

2 ribs celery, sliced on the bias into ¼-inch pieces

4 medium carrots, peeled and cut on the bias into ¼-inch pieces

2 cups low-sodium chicken stock

6 tablespoons unsalted butter

¼ cup all-purpose flour

2 tablespoons good-quality Hungarian paprika

1 teaspoon minced garlic

½ cup sour cream (not low-fat)

Serves 6

Preheat the oven to 350 degrees.

Season the chicken with salt and pepper. Place in a roasting pan, add the water, and cook, uncovered, for 1 hour. Cool slightly, then break the chicken into large pieces with your hands. Return to the pan and set aside.

As the chicken cooks, prepare the sauce. In a large, deep skillet or Dutch oven, heat the oil over medium–high heat. Add the onions, celery, and carrots. Season with salt and pepper and cook until the onions are soft, 5 to 7 minutes. Add the chicken stock, bring to a boil, reduce to a simmer, and cook until the vegetables are tender, about 10 minutes.

In a medium saucepan, melt the butter over medium–low heat. Add the flour and whisk until a smooth paste forms. Reduce the heat to low, add the paprika, and cook, whisking constantly, for 1 minute.

Whisk the hot roux into the simmering vegetables. Simmer for 10 minutes, stirring often to prevent scorching. Add the garlic and cooked chicken meat, along with any accumulated juices from the pan; simmer for 10 more minutes, stirring often. Reduce the heat to low and add the sour cream, gently stirring until incorporated (do not boil, or the sour cream will curdle). Add enough stock, if needed, to make the sauce the consistency of a loose gravy. Season with salt and pepper to taste and serve.

Seasoned salt

2 tablespoons kosher salt

2 teaspoons sugar

¾ teaspoon paprika

¼ teaspoon ground turmeric

¼ teaspoon onion powder

¼ teaspoon garlic powder

Garlic salt

1 tablespoon kosher salt

1 teaspoon garlic powder

Pork

One (2- to 4-pound) boneless
   pork loin roast

Up to 2 teaspoons garlic salt

Up to 2 teaspoons seasoned salt

Serves 6 to 12

Legendary Pork Loin from the Ohio State Fair

OHIO PORK COUNCIL, COLUMBUS
FARMERS KENNY AND JANET STIVERSON

Ohio has the third-highest number of pork farms in the United States. A good-quality pork loin, simply prepared, is always amazingly good. The key is to not overcook it; grilled or roasted, it should still have a blush of pink at its center. Kenny and Janet are hog farmers who cook and sell this dish at the Ohio State Fair in Columbus every year—it's their signature recipe. You can use store-bought seasoned salt (such as Lawry's), or use the recipe here to blend your own.

If making your own seasoned salt or garlic salt, combine the salt and seasonings together in a small bowl and set aside.

Rub the pork with ½ teaspoon each of the garlic salt and seasoned salt per pound. The pork may be refrigerated like this, uncovered, for up to 4 hours. Whether grilling or roasting, remove the pork from the refrigerator 30 minutes before cooking to let it reach room temperature.

Grilling method:
Prepare a grill for indirect grilling, with the fire on one side and the heat on the other. When the coals are glowing and covered with white ash, bank them on one side of the grill. Put the pork on the side opposite the fire and close the lid (the target temperature for the grill is 300 to 350 degrees). Cook for 30 minutes. Check the temperature with a probe thermometer and continue grilling until the internal temperature of the pork is 145 degrees. If the outside of the pork is getting dark but the inside temperature is not 145 degrees, loosely tent the pork in foil and continue cooking. The average cooking time is an hour or longer. When the pork is at 145 degrees, let it rest for 3 minutes before slicing.

Roasting method:

Preheat the oven to 350 degrees. (If you have a convection setting on your oven, use it.)

Place the pork in a shallow, rimmed pan and roast for about 45 minutes (15 minutes per pound), or until an instant-read thermometer registers 145 degrees. Start checking the temperature of the meat after 30 minutes. Remove the roast from the oven and let it rest for 3 minutes before slicing to serve.

2 large boneless, skinless
chicken breasts

½ cup plain yogurt, preferably
whole milk (such as
Snowville Creamery's
6 percent plain)

1 teaspoon freshly squeezed
lemon juice

¼ teaspoon finely grated
lemon zest

1 teaspoon grated fresh ginger
or 1 tablespoon minced
candied ginger

⅛ teaspoon freshly ground
black pepper

Salt

⅓ cup finely diced celery

⅓ cup finely diced crisp and
tart apple, such as Pinova
or Granny Smith

⅓ cup halved green grapes

4 tablespoons toasted slivered
almonds, divided

Fresh leaves of head lettuce
(optional)

Serves 4

Lemon Ginger Yogurt Chicken Salad

SNOWVILLE CREAMERY, POMEROY ❧ ARIEL TAYLOR

Snowville Creamery's grass-fed cows and lower-heat pasteurization method result in milk that retains more of its natural flavor. The difference is eye-opening, and it's why customers in Ohio seek out Snowville products, including their lusciously creamy yogurt. It's the base for the dressing in this satisfying and refreshing chicken salad. The recipe comes from Ariel Taylor, niece of Snowville founders Warren and Victoria Taylor.

Bring a large saucepan of heavily salted water to a very low boil. Add the chicken breasts, cover, and cook until the chicken registers 165 degrees on an instant-read thermometer. Drain, set on a plate to cool, and then chill in the refrigerator until cold.

In a large bowl, combine the yogurt, lemon juice, lemon zest, ginger, pepper, and salt. Dice the poached chicken (you should have about 4 cups) and add to the bowl. Fold with a rubber spatula until the chicken is coated evenly, then fold in the celery, apples, grapes, and 2 tablespoons of the almonds. Taste and adjust seasoning with more salt, pepper, or lemon juice, if necessary.

Divide the lettuce, if using, between serving plates and top with scoops of chicken salad. Sprinkle the remaining 2 tablespoons almonds on top and serve immediately. The salad is best enjoyed shortly after making it, but leftovers will keep, refrigerated, for up to 3 days.

❧ *Note: You may substitute Snowville Creamery Lemon Ginger Yogurt for the plain yogurt and omit the lemon juice, lemon zest, and ginger. Also, instead of poaching the chicken, you may use 4 cups of diced, chilled meat from a rotisserie chicken. To toast the almonds, place on a rimmed baking sheet and bake at 350 degrees until fragrant and lightly browned, about 5 minutes.*

Spring garlic and mushrooms

3 tablespoons olive oil

1 portabello mushroom, chopped

3 shiitake mushroom caps, chopped

3 stalks spring garlic, white and light green parts only, thinly sliced

2 tablespoons unsalted butter

1 shallot, finely diced

Salt and freshly ground black pepper

Orzo risotto

4 cups low-sodium chicken stock

1½ tablespoons olive oil

1 small onion, finely diced

1 cup uncooked orzo pasta

1½ tablespoons truffle butter

1 ounce (½ cup) grated Parmesan cheese

2½ cups loosely packed baby arugula leaves

1½ tablespoons heavy cream

Parmesan cheese, thinly shaved with a vegetable peeler, for garnish

Serves 4

Orzo Risotto with Spring Garlic and Forest Mushrooms

DANTE, CLEVELAND ❧ CHEF DANTE BOCCUZZI

Lots of stirring as it cooks makes this orzo creamy, just like a risotto. The cream folded in at the end gives it an especially silky texture. Spring garlic is just immature garlic, seasonally available from March through May. It's a thin stalk that hasn't yet formed a bulb, with a milder flavor than mature garlic. Prepare it as you would a scallion (which it resembles, physically), and save the darker green tops for stock.

For the spring garlic and mushrooms:
Set a large skillet over medium-high heat and add the olive oil. When it shimmers, add the mushrooms and spring garlic and cook until golden brown, 5 minutes. Add the butter and shallots and cook until the butter browns and the shallots are translucent, 3 to 5 minutes. Season with salt and black pepper. Set aside and keep warm.

For the orzo risotto:
In a medium saucepan, bring the stock to a low simmer. Cover and keep hot.

In a high-sided skillet over medium heat, heat the olive oil. Add the onions and cook until translucent and tender, 6 to 8 minutes. Add the orzo and stir until coated with oil. Add enough simmering stock to cover the pasta. Stir constantly, reducing the heat as needed to keep a low simmer. Continue stirring and adding stock about 1 cup at a time until the orzo is just firm to the bite (you may not need all the stock). Add the truffle butter, Parmesan cheese, and baby arugula. Taste and adjust seasoning with salt and pepper.

In a small chilled bowl, whisk the cream until thick and somewhat fluffy. With a heat-safe spatula, fold the cream into the orzo. Divide the orzo between serving bowls; top with the mushrooms and garlic. Garnish with the Parmesan cheese shavings and serve immediately.

❧ **Note:** *Truffle butter is a compound butter flavored with minced black truffles. It's available at gourmet food markets or online. If you can't find spring garlic, substitute two thinly sliced cloves of regular garlic.*

Kraut spice mix

1 tablespoon kosher salt

1 tablespoon ground black pepper

2 tablespoons celery seed

1 ½ teaspoons ground coriander seed

2 tablespoons caraway seed

¾ teaspoon chili powder

3 tablespoons brown sugar

Vodka kraut

1 teaspoon vegetable oil

½ small onion, diced

1 cup loosely packed chopped napa cabbage

1 tablespoon kraut spice mix

2 tablespoons vodka

2 tablespoons apple cider vinegar

Parmageddon

MELT BAR & GRILLED, LAKEWOOD
OWNER AND FOUNDER MATTHEW FISH

Grilled cheese is the name of the game at Melt, an Ohio-bred chain offering clever variations on the comfort food classic, from basic to outrageous. This sandwich—loaded with browned pierogi and cabbage quickly sautéed with spices and a splash of vodka—falls in the latter category. It might sound like carb overload on paper, but the vodka kraut adds a bracing crunch, making the towering sandwich lighter than you'd imagine. You can use store-bought pierogi or the homemade ones in this chapter (see page 114).

For the kraut spice mix:
Combine all the ingredients in a small bowl and whisk to mix.

For the vodka kraut:
In a small skillet, heat the oil over medium–high heat. Add the onions and cook until soft and beginning to brown, 4 to 6 minutes. Add the cabbage, kraut spice, vodka, and vinegar and cook until the liquid is nearly evaporated. Set aside; keep warm.

For assembly:
Heat the vegetable oil in another small skillet over medium heat. Add the frozen pierogi and cook until golden brown and crispy on both sides, 5 to 10 minutes per side. Drain on paper towels and keep warm.

Preheat the broiler. Butter both sides of each bread slice and either toast or broil until lightly golden brown at the edges.

Put the toasted bread on a baking sheet. Place two slices of cheese on each bread slice. Top the cheese on one bread slice with the seared pierogi, and top the cheese on the other bread slice with the cooked

Assembly

1 tablespoon vegetable oil

2 frozen potato and Cheddar pierogi, purchased or homemade (*see page 114*)

2 thick slices of good white sandwich bread

Softened butter, for spreading

4 slices Cheddar cheese

2 sandwich picks or sturdy toothpicks

Makes 1 sandwich

vodka kraut. Broil, watching carefully that the bread does not burn, until the cheese melts, about 45 seconds. Remove from the broiler, close the sandwich, and secure with two sandwich picks or tooth-picks placed near opposite corners. Cut into two triangular halves and serve immediately.

❧ **Note:** *The kraut spice mix will keep, tightly covered in a jar, for 6 months. If you prefer, you may deep-fry the frozen pierogi instead of cooking them in a skillet. Heat 3 inches of vegetable oil to 350 degrees, add the frozen pierogi, and fry until they float to the surface and are golden brown and a little blistered, about 4 minutes.*

Filling

2 pounds (about 6 medium)
    unpeeled Yukon gold potatoes,
    cut into 2-inch chunks

½ cup milk

8 ounces (2 cups) grated sharp
    Cheddar cheese

Salt and freshly ground
    black pepper

Dough

4⅓ cups all-purpose flour,
    plus more for dusting

1¼ teaspoons kosher salt

1 cup cold water

⅓ cup sour cream

1 egg

1 tablespoon canola oil

For serving

½ cup (1 stick) salted butter

1 to 2 large onions, finely diced

Sour cream

Fresh chives or dill, chopped

Makes 2 to 3 dozen large pierogi

Potato and Cheddar Pierogi

SOKOLOWSKI'S UNIVERSITY INN, CLEVELAND
CO-OWNER MICHAEL SOKOLOWSKI

*Like many beloved old-world foods, pierogi take some work. But they are
fun to make, especially when you enlist friends and family to help roll,
cut, and fill the dough. This recipe makes a lot, but you can cook some
and freeze the rest to enjoy later.*

For the filling:

A day before you plan to shape the pierogi, make the filling. Place
the potatoes in a medium saucepan and cover with cold water.
Season with salt. Bring to a boil, reduce to a simmer, and cook
until the potatoes are tender, 10 to 12 minutes. Drain, return to the
pot, and mash with a potato masher (keep the skins on; they add
a nice texture to the filling). Add the milk and mix until combined.
Add the cheese, along with salt and pepper. Taste and add more
salt and pepper, if needed; the mixture should be quite seasoned.
Transfer to a medium bowl, let cool a bit, and chill until cool
and firm.

For the dough and to assemble:

In the bowl of an electric stand mixer fitted with a dough hook,
combine the flour and salt. In a glass measuring cup, lightly beat
together the water, sour cream, egg, and oil. Add to the flour
mixture and mix for about 5 minutes. The dough should be soft
and springy. If it's sticky, add a little more flour; if it's stiff, add
a little more water. Remove the dough from the bowl and let
it rest, covered, on a lightly floured counter for about 30 minutes.

Divide the dough in half. With a floured rolling pin, roll out to
¼-inch thickness. Cut into circles with a 4-inch round cutter or
drinking glass. Take a circle and roll it out to a ⅛-inch thickness
(about 5 to 6 inches in diameter). Add a rounded tablespoon of

the chilled filling to the center. Lightly wet one edge of the dough with water, fold it over to make a half-moon, and firmly crimp the edges with a fork. Place on a floured tray. Repeat with the remaining circles. Keep the shaped pierogi covered with a lint-free tea towel as you roll out, shape, and fill the remaining dough.

To cook and serve the pierogi:
Melt the butter in a 12-inch skillet over medium heat. Add the onions and cook until very soft and just beginning to brown, about 10 minutes.

Bring a large pot of salted water to just below boiling (about 190 degrees). Add the pierogi in batches and cook until they float to the surface, about 3 minutes. Remove with a slotted spoon or skimmer. Add to the skillet and, in batches, slowly brown in the butter (don't jostle them too much or they will break), about 8 minutes per side. Serve with sour cream and chopped fresh chives or dill.

❧ **Note:** *You can use many kinds of fillings in the dough—potato and Cheddar are just a starting point. What's important is that the filling is not runny, or it will be difficult to shape and crimp the pierogi. You can freeze the shaped but uncooked pierogi for up to 3 months. Lay them out on a greased baking sheet and freeze until firm (about 2 hours) before transferring to a zip-top freezer bag. To prepare, add the frozen pierogi to gently boiling water and simply cook for a few minutes longer than you would fresh pierogi.*

Walleye

3¾ ounces (1 sleeve) buttery
   round crackers, such as Ritz

2 large eggs

1 cup milk

1 cup all-purpose flour

4 skinned and boned walleye fillets,
   about 6 ounces each

Kosher salt

Canola oil, for frying

Shallot cream sauce

1½ tablespoons whole black
   peppercorns

½ cup dry white wine

½ cup sherry (sweet or dry)

2 tablespoons minced shallots

¼ cup clam juice

¾ cup heavy cream

¼ teaspoon roasted garlic

1 teaspoon cornstarch

⅛ to ¼ teaspoon Tabasco™
   or other hot red pepper sauce

¼ teaspoon freshly squeezed
   lemon juice

Salt

Ritz-Crusted Walleye with Crab and Shallot Cream Sauce

CAMERON'S AMERICAN BISTRO, COLUMBUS
REGIONAL CHEF PETER CHAPMAN

Walleye is Ohio's state fish and also one of the most coveted game fish in the Midwest. Once found in a number of Ohio's rivers, walleye is still abundant in Lake Erie. It is prized for its mildly sweet flavor and meaty yet delicate texture, which here is complemented by a fine golden crust of ground Ritz crackers.

To bread the walleye:
Grind the crackers in a food processor fitted with a steel blade until they are sandy and fine. You should have about a cup. Place in a large, shallow bowl or a plate with a high rim.

Whisk together the eggs and milk; set aside. Place the flour in a large, shallow bowl or plate with a high rim. Season both sides of the fish with kosher salt. Dredge a fillet in flour and gently shake to remove excess. Dip the fillet in the egg mixture, then place in the cracker crumbs, gently pressing crumbs on all sides of the fish to make sure they stick. Lay on a tray and repeat with the remaining fillets. Let rest for an hour in the refrigerator (this helps make a crispy crust during frying).

For the shallot cream sauce:
In a small, dry skillet, toast the peppercorns over medium heat until fragrant. Pulse in a spice grinder until cracked but not finely ground (or chop them on a cutting board with a sharp knife). Set aside.

In a medium saucepan, combine the white wine, sherry, shallots, and cracked pepper. Bring to a boil and cook on high heat until syrupy. Add the clam stock and reduce by half. Add the heavy cream, reduce heat to medium, and simmer for 5 minutes. Add

Crab

4 tablespoons unsalted butter

4 ounces lump crab meat,
   picked over

Chopped fresh parsley, for garnish

Serves 4

the roasted garlic. Combine the cornstarch in a small bowl with 1 teaspoon water, then add it to the simmering sauce and stir until slightly thickened. Remove from heat and add the Tabasco™, lemon juice, and salt to taste. Keep warm.

For the crab:
Melt the butter in a medium skillet over low heat. Add the crab to warm it through.

To fry the fish and serve:
In a large skillet (cast iron works well), add enough oil to reach halfway up the sides of the fish. Heat over medium–high. When a small piece of bread browns nicely in a minute or so, the oil is ready. Carefully add half the fish and fry until the sides are golden, 1 to 3 minutes. Flip over and cook for 1 to 3 minutes more, until golden on both sides. Remove from oil and set on a plate lined with paper towels to drain. Repeat with remaining fish.

Right before serving, add a pinch of parsley to the crab. To serve, place a spoonful of the cream sauce on a plate, place the walleye in the middle of the sauce, and top with crab. Sprinkle lightly with the remaining parsley and serve.

Herb crust

¼ cup chopped fresh parsley

2 tablespoons chopped fresh thyme

2 tablespoons chopped fresh oregano

½ cup (1 stick) unsalted butter, softened

1 teaspoon kosher salt

1 cup panko bread crumbs

Red wine sauce

4 cups dry red wine

¼ cup sugar

1 cup white mushrooms, cleaned

4 cups low-sodium beef stock

2 thyme sprigs

1 bay leaf

5 whole black peppercorns

4 tablespoons unsalted butter

Salt and freshly ground black pepper

Potato puree

1 cup heavy cream

½ cup (1 stick) unsalted butter

1 pound russet potatoes, peeled and cut into chunks

Salt and freshly ground white pepper

Roasted Bone-in Rib Eye, Herb Crust, Potato Puree, and Red Wine Sauce

ORCHIDS AT PALM COURT, CINCINNATI
EXECUTIVE CHEF TODD KELLY

Award-winning chef Todd Kelly has created a national reputation with his fine-dining restaurant in Cincinnati's Hilton Netherland Plaza hotel, earning an American Culinary Federation Chef of the Year award in 2011. The ingenious crust on this rib eye is more like a compound butter studded with crunchy bread crumbs. Simple to make in advance, it elevates a good steak into an amazing presentation with lively flavors and textures.

For the herb crust:
Combine all the ingredients and roll between two pieces of parchment paper to an even ⅛-inch thickness. Slide the parchment onto a plate and freeze until firm but slightly pliable, about 30 minutes. Once frozen, cut into circles that are slightly smaller than the widest part of the rib eyes. (If you don't have a round cutter, use a drinking glass as a guide; gently press the glass into the butter mixture to leave an impression, then cut out the circle with a paring knife.) Return the circles to the freezer until needed.

For the red wine sauce:
Bring the wine and sugar to a boil in a medium saucepan. Reduce the heat slightly and simmer until reduced by half. Add the mushrooms, beef stock, thyme sprigs, bay leaf, and peppercorns and simmer until slightly syrupy (you will have about ⅓ cup). Strain and discard the solids. Over low heat, whisk in the butter. Season with salt and pepper. Keep warm, but do not boil.

Rib eyes

4 (10-ounce) beef rib eye steaks
(bone-in if possible)

Salt and freshly ground
black pepper

1 tablespoon canola oil

Serves 4

For the potato puree:
Heat the cream and butter in a small saucepan over low heat and keep warm. Place the potatoes in a medium saucepan and add water to cover. Season heavily with salt. Bring to a boil, reduce to a simmer, and cook until tender. Drain. Immediately transfer the cooked potatoes to a blender. With the blender running, add the warm cream and butter in a thin stream until the potatoes are smooth. (If you let the potatoes cool a bit, they become gluey in the blender, so work quickly.) Season with salt and white pepper to taste. Keep warm.

To cook the rib eyes and finish:
Preheat the broiler. Season the rib eyes with salt and pepper.

Heat a large skillet, preferably cast iron, over high heat. Add the oil. When it shimmers, add the steaks. Cook until nicely seared, about 3 minutes per side. Set the cooked steaks on a rimmed baking sheet. Place a disk of the herb crust on top of each rib eye. Broil until the herb crust is golden brown, about 3 minutes (don't leave the broiler unattended; the crust can burn in a matter of seconds).

Place a large spoonful of the potato puree on a plate and drizzle the sauce around the puree. Place the steak on top of the puree. Garnish with cooked seasonal vegetables.

✺ **Note:** *Chef Kelly uses bone-in rib eye steaks, but they can be hard to find in sizes small enough for single portions. You can use boneless rib eyes instead, as we did in the photo. The change only slightly reduces the cooking time. If you have leftover herb crust, use it to top cooked grilled chicken or fish, or crumble it frozen onto a casserole before baking for a buttery, crunchy topping.*

Short pastry

3 cups all-purpose flour

3 tablespoons plus 1 teaspoon sugar

⅛ teaspoon salt

1 cup (2 sticks) plus 3 tablespoons unsalted butter, cut into 1-inch cubes and briefly frozen

1 egg yolk

⅓ cup cold water

Curry potatoes

1 tablespoon plus 1 teaspoon peanut oil

Pinch cumin seed

1 large Anaheim pepper, seeded and diced

1 tablespoon minced fresh ginger

¼ cup water

¼ teaspoon ground turmeric

¼ teaspoon chili powder

¾ teaspoon ground coriander

¾ teaspoon ground cumin

½ teaspoon salt

½ teaspoon sugar

2 medium russet potatoes, peeled and cut into large chunks

Vegetable gravy

2 tablespoons plus 2 teaspoons vegetable oil

1 small onion, finely diced

2 garlic cloves, minced

3 tablespoons all-purpose flour

Roasted Veggie Pot Pie

O PIE O, CINCINNATI ❧ CHEF PAUL ALFORD

You've never had a pot pie like this before. Using different cooking techniques to prepare the vegetables for the filling results in unexpected layers of flavor and texture. You're best off making the pastry, fillings, and gravy a day in advance, and baking and assembling the pie the following day.

For the short pastry:
In a food processor fitted with a steel blade, pulse the flour, sugar, and salt. Add the butter and egg yolk, and pulse until the butter chunks are pea-sized. Add the water and pulse a few times until the dough clumps up. Remove and knead lightly.

Weigh out a 14-ounce piece and an 11-ounce piece; form each into round discs. Wrap in plastic wrap and refrigerate for 1 hour.

Roll the large disc into a 14-inch circle and place into a deep 9-inch pie plate. Trim any excess dough. Roll the small disc into a 12-inch circle. Slide a small cookie sheet under the small dough circle. Cover both crusts with plastic wrap and return to the refrigerator.

For the curry potatoes:
In a medium skillet, heat the oil and cumin seeds over medium heat until the seeds start to crackle. Add the peppers and ginger and cook until the peppers are tender, 3 minutes. Add the water, remaining spices, salt, and sugar and simmer for 5 minutes. Add the potatoes, cover, and cook, stirring occasionally, until the potatoes are tender, 10 to 20 minutes (add a little water if the potatoes start to stick). Remove and set aside to cool.

For the vegetable gravy:
In a medium pan, heat the oil over medium heat. Add the onions and cook until transparent, 6 minutes. Add the garlic and cook another 1 to 2 minutes. Mix in the flour to create a smooth paste. Slowly whisk in the broth. Add the nutritional yeast, soy sauce, salt, and pepper and simmer for 1 minute. Scrape into a large bowl to cool.

1 ½ cups low-sodium vegetable broth

1 ¼ teaspoons nutritional yeast

1 tablespoon plus 1 teaspoon
    soy sauce

⅛ teaspoon salt

⅛ teaspoon freshly ground
    black pepper

Roasted cauliflower

¼ cup extra-virgin olive oil

5 garlic cloves, minced

¼ teaspoon red pepper flakes

½ teaspoon kosher salt

2 teaspoons dried thyme

1 head cauliflower,
    cut into bite-size pieces

Sautéed vegetables

2 tablespoons vegetable oil

1 medium carrot, peeled and
    cut into coins

1 bunch scallions, sliced

4 ounces white or shiitake
    mushrooms, sliced

Egg wash

1 egg beaten with 1 tablespoon
    water

Serves 4 to 6

For the roasted cauliflower:
Preheat the oven to 350 degrees.

Whisk the oil, garlic, red pepper, salt, and thyme in a large bowl. Add the cauliflower and toss to thoroughly coat. Spread evenly on a parchment-lined rimmed baking sheet and roast until the smallest pieces are dark and crispy, 20 to 30 minutes.

For the sautéed vegetables:
Heat the oil in a medium skillet over medium-high heat. Add the carrots and cook until lightly browned, about 3 minutes. Add the scallions and mushrooms and cook until the mushrooms are lightly browned, about 5 minutes. Set aside to cool.

To assemble and bake:
In a large bowl, combine the gravy, potatoes, cauliflower, and sautéed vegetables. Scrape into the pastry-lined pie dish and smooth to make a dome. Cover with the top pastry and crimp the edges together. Brush with the egg wash. Freeze for at least 1 hour.

Preheat the oven to 375 degrees. Bake the pie for 40 to 60 minutes, rotating halfway through, until the entire top crust is a nice brown color. Reduce to 300 degrees and continue to bake until an instant-read thermometer inserted just under the center of the top crust registers above 135 degrees. Let the pie rest for at least 10 minutes before cutting and serving.

❧ *Note: The assembled, unbaked pie may be frozen for up to 1 month.*

3 pounds Yukon gold potatoes,
   peeled and diced

½ teaspoon salt

½ teaspoon freshly ground
   black pepper

4 tablespoons unsalted butter,
   cut into small pieces

2 cups sauerkraut, drained
   and rinsed

1 cup sour cream

1 cup finely shredded
   Cheddar cheese

8 slices bacon, cooked
   and crumbled

4 to 6 pimento-stuffed green olives

Serves 4 to 6

Sauerkraut German Sundae

OHIO SAUERKRAUT FESTIVAL, WAYNESVILLE

Every October, the Ohio Sauerkraut Festival features fermented cabbage in all its glory. Food vendors work kraut into every conceivable dish, including sauerkraut pizza and sauerkraut fudge, but this appealing concoction is the festival's must-try item. It hits the spot in cooler weather, and you can tailor the amount of toppings to your own taste.

Preheat the oven to 350 degrees. Toss the potatoes with the salt and pepper in a 9 x 13–inch baking pan. Dot with the butter, cover with foil, and bake until the potatoes are tender but not falling apart, 30 to 45 minutes.

Meanwhile, bring the sauerkraut to a simmer in a medium saucepan. Reduce the heat to just keep it warm.

For each serving, put about a cup of the cooked potatoes in a bowl. Top with as much sauerkraut as you like (¼ to ½ cup is good), then add 2 tablespoons of the sour cream, then ¼ cup Cheddar cheese, then 1 tablespoon crumbled bacon. Garnish with a single olive and serve immediately.

3 tablespoons olive oil, divided

1 large onion, chopped

5 garlic cloves, minced

1 green bell pepper, seeded and cored, finely diced

12 ounces crimini mushrooms, cleaned and chopped

1½ pounds lean ground beef (90/10 is good)

1 (28-ounce) can whole plum tomatoes in juice, crushed

3 tablespoons tomato paste

¾ teaspoon dried oregano

¼ teaspoon crushed red pepper flakes

Salt and freshly ground black pepper

2¾ cups (12 ounces) uncooked elbow macaroni

8 ounces (2 generous cups) grated sharp Cheddar cheese, divided

6 ounces (1½ cups) grated Parmesan cheese, divided

Serves 8

21st Century Johnny Marzetti

SARA BIR, THE SAUSAGETARIAN

Hearty ground beef and pasta casseroles are fixtures of Midwestern cooking, but this notable entry in the genre has a distinctive origin story. Italian immigrant Teresa Marzetti opened a restaurant close to the Ohio State University campus in 1896. She created this filling dish for cash-strapped college students and named it after her brother-in-law. The last of Marzetti's restaurants closed in 1972, but today home cooks still make their own versions of this casserole. This one takes the essence of the original and amps up the flavors to better suit today's palates for Ohio-born comfort food at its finest.

Preheat the oven to 350 degrees. Grease a 9 x 13-inch baking dish.

Heat 1 tablespoon of the olive oil in a large skillet over medium-high heat. Add the onions and cook until translucent, about 6 minutes. Add the garlic and bell pepper and cook for 1 minute. Season with salt and scrape into a large bowl; set aside. Return the skillet to the heat. Add the remaining 2 tablespoons olive oil. Add the mushrooms, stirring occasionally, and cook until browned, about 5 minutes. Season with salt and scrape into the bowl with the onion mixture. Return the skillet to the heat and add the beef. Reduce heat to medium and cook, breaking the beef into smaller clumps with a spoon, until no longer pink, about 8 minutes. Spoon off most of the fat and liquid, if any has accumulated, and discard. Add the tomatoes, tomato paste, oregano, and red pepper flakes and simmer until saucy, about 20 minutes. Add the reserved onion-mushroom mixture and simmer for 2 more minutes. Season to taste with salt and pepper.

Meanwhile, bring a large pot of salted water to boil. Add the elbow macaroni and cook until al dente. Drain and return the macaroni to the pot. Add the cooked sauce and toss. Mix in half of the cheeses. Turn into the greased baking dish and scatter the remaining grated cheese on top. Bake until the sauce is bubbling and the cheese is lightly browned, about 30 minutes. Let rest for 10 minutes before serving.

Desserts & Sweet Treats

Date cake

Butter or cooking spray

1 cup chopped pitted dates

1 tablespoon unsalted butter

1 teaspoon baking soda

1 cup very hot water

1 cup granulated sugar

1 large egg, slightly beaten

1 teaspoon vanilla extract

½ teaspoon salt

1 cup all-purpose flour

½ cup chopped walnuts or pecans

Butterscotch sauce

¾ cup brown sugar

3 tablespoons Clear Jel
(not instant; *see Note*)

Pinch salt

1½ cups water

2 tablespoons unsalted butter

¾ teaspoon vanilla extract

½ teaspoon maple flavor

To assemble

2 cups heavy cream, whipped

Serves 8 to 12

Amish Date Pudding

THE BARN INN BED AND BREAKFAST, MILLERSBURG
INNKEEPER LORETTA COBLENTZ

Coblentz, who comes from an Amish background, says this dessert is frequently served at Amish weddings. It's more like a rustic trifle made of cubed date cake than it is a pudding. Some versions fold the cake cubes with whipped cream and serve it in one large communal bowl. Coblentz layers hers in individual dishes for a more refined presentation.

For the date cake:

Preheat the oven to 350 degrees. Line a 13 x 9-inch pan with parchment. Grease the sides and the parchment with butter or cooking spray.

In a large bowl, combine the dates, butter, soda, and hot water; stir until the butter is melted. Stir in the sugar, egg, vanilla, salt, flour, and nuts (the batter will be thin). Pour the batter into the parchment-lined pan and bake until the center of the cake is firm to the touch and the sides pull away from the pan, 35 to 45 minutes. Cool on a wire rack for 10 minutes, then invert, peel off the parchment, flip over again, and cool completely.

For the butterscotch sauce:

In a medium saucepan, combine the brown sugar, Clear Jel, and salt. Add the water and butter. Cook over medium heat, stirring constantly with a rubber spatula, until the sauce thickens, about 5 minutes. Remove from heat and stir in the vanilla and maple flavor. Scrape into a small bowl or large glass measuring cup and let cool. Cover and refrigerate until needed.

To assemble:

Cut the cooled cake into small cubes (this is easiest to do when the cake is chilled).

Layer the pudding either in a large bowl or trifle dish, or in individual ramekins or dessert dishes. Begin with a layer of cake cubes, then top with a layer of whipped cream, then a drizzle of butterscotch sauce. Repeat, ending with whipped cream on top. Serve immediately.

❧ **Note:** *For convenience, you may bake the cake in advance, cube it, and freeze it in individual portions. Clear Jel is a modified cornstarch that Amish and Mennonite cooks use to thicken many of their pies and sauces. Its thickening ability is more tolerant of heat and freezing than regular cornstarch. It can be obtained from any Amish bulk food store.*

Anne's Apple Fer

BAR DUMAINE, DAYTON   CHEF-OWNER ANNE KEARNEY

This epic dessert is stunning straight from the skillet. A riff on Far Breton cake, it's somewhere between a flan and a clafoutis. Apples sautéed in butter and deglazed with brandy rest in an oozy, caramelized sauce. Perfect for dessert lovers who aren't keen on the finer points of baking pastries or cakes, it's typical of Chef Kearney's French-influenced fare.

1 tablespoon unsalted butter

4 tart and firm apples,
    cored and peeled

¼ cup golden raisins

4 tablespoons Armagnac
    or other brandy, divided

Salt and freshly ground white pepper

1¼ cups granulated sugar, divided

1 cup firmly packed light
    brown sugar

½ cup water

3 cups milk

5 large eggs

1¼ cups plus 2 tablespoons
    all-purpose flour

4½ teaspoons vanilla extract

Powdered sugar (optional)

Sweetened whipped cream
    or ice cream, for serving

Sprigs of fresh mint, for garnish

Serves 16

Melt the butter over medium heat in a 12-inch cast-iron pan with high sides. Add the apples and cook until golden brown, 5 to 10 minutes, turning as they brown. Stir in the raisins and 2 tablespoons of the Armagnac and cook, stirring gently, for 2 minutes. Season gently with salt, scrape into a medium bowl, and set aside.

In the same pan, combine ½ cup of the granulated sugar, the brown sugar, water, and the remaining 2 tablespoons Armagnac. Season with salt and a few grinds of white pepper. Bring to a boil over high heat, then reduce the heat to medium and cook, stirring occasionally, until the liquid reduces by half and becomes syrupy, 10 to 15 minutes. Remove from heat. Scatter the apples and raisins around the pan, along with any juices. Let sit while you make the batter.

Preheat the oven to 350 degrees. In a large mixing bowl, whisk together the milk, eggs, the remaining ¾ cup granulated sugar, flour, and vanilla until smooth. Strain the batter through a fine-mesh sieve over the apple and caramel mixture. Bake until the center sets, 1 to 1½ hours.

Remove the pan from the oven and cool for 20 minutes. Dust lightly with powdered sugar, if desired. Take this gorgeous dessert to the table and serve right from the pan with whipped cream or ice cream, plus a garnish of mint sprigs.

  ❧ **Note:** *If you don't have a 12-inch skillet, you can halve the recipe, but use three eggs and make it in a deep 10-inch skillet. Adjust the baking time to 30 to 45 minutes. The halved apple fer will serve 8 people.*

1 cup plus 2 tablespoons heavy cream, divided

7 ounces semisweet chocolate (around 60 percent cacao), finely chopped

3 egg yolks

3 egg whites

½ cup sugar

Serves 8

Belgian Chocolate Mousse

THE REFECTORY, COLUMBUS   &   CHEF RICHARD BLONDIN

Fancy chocolate desserts come and go, but one taste of this ethereal mousse and you'll see why some things never go out of style. While individual dishes make serving easy, the mousse retains more of its seductive, light texture when you put it in one large dish.

In a medium bowl, whip 1 cup minus 1 tablespoon of the heavy cream to soft peaks and refrigerate until ready to use.

Combine the chocolate and the remaining 3 tablespoons heavy cream in a medium heat-safe bowl over a pan of barely simmering water. Stir with a heat-safe spatula until melted and smooth. Remove the bowl from heat and stir in the egg yolks. (If the chocolate mixture seizes and becomes greasy, stir in 1 tablespoon cold water and the mixture will gradually become smooth again.) Scrape into a large, clean bowl and fold in the reserved whipped cream.

In a large, grease-free bowl, beat the egg whites and the sugar until stiff and glossy peaks form. Fold the beaten egg whites into the bowl with the chocolate mixture until no streaks remain.

Transfer to a 1½- to 2-quart soufflé dish or into eight individual dessert dishes, and refrigerate for a minimum of 8 hours before serving.

& *Note: This contains raw eggs, and so is not suitable for young children, pregnant women, the elderly, or those with compromised immune systems. Use locally raised farm eggs, if possible. With so few ingredients, using good-quality semisweet chocolate is imperative. Don't use chocolate with a cacao content higher than 65 percent in this recipe, because the chocolate will seize up when you fold in the egg yolks.*

Brown Sugar Cookies

MURPHIN RIDGE INN, WEST UNION   OWNER PAULA SCHUTT

Murphin Ridge Inn sits on 142 acres in Adams County, not far from the Great Serpent Mound. These simple drop cookies show the local Amish influence. Soft and with a penuche-like cooked icing, they're excellent with a cup of tea.

Cookies

3 ¼ cups all-purpose flour

2 teaspoons baking powder

½ teaspoon baking soda

½ teaspoon salt

1 cup (2 sticks) unsalted butter, room temperature

2 cups light brown sugar

2 large eggs

½ cup milk

1 teaspoon vanilla extract

Icing

3 tablespoons unsalted butter

3 tablespoons half-and-half or whole milk, plus more if needed

½ cup light brown sugar

¾ cup powdered sugar, plus more if needed

Makes 2½ dozen cookies

For the cookies:

Preheat the oven to 375 degrees with racks in the upper and lower thirds of the oven. Line two baking sheets with parchment or silicone baking mats.

In a medium bowl, whisk together the flour, baking powder, baking soda, and salt. Set aside.

In the bowl of an electric mixer fitted with the paddle attachment, beat the butter and sugar until fluffy. Add the eggs one at a time, scraping down the bowl after each addition. Slowly beat in the milk and vanilla, followed by the flour mixture. The batter will be sticky.

Drop by tablespoons onto the prepared baking sheets, twelve to a sheet. Bake until lightly browned and set in the centers, about 12 minutes, rotating the pans from top to bottom and back to front halfway through baking. Let the cookies cool on the sheets for a few minutes before transferring to wire racks with a metal spatula.

For the icing:

While the cookies cool, combine the butter, half-and-half or milk, and brown sugar in a small saucepan over medium-high heat. Bring to a boil, whisking constantly, and boil for 1 minute. Remove from heat and beat in the powdered sugar. The icing should be smooth and spreadable; add a little powdered sugar or half-and-half, if needed. Working quickly, frost the cookies with a small metal spatula while the icing is still warm. If it begins to get grainy or set up, return the pan to the burner and warm gently over medium-low heat.

The cookies will keep in a covered container for 3 days, if they don't instantly disappear.

Custard

1 ¼ teaspoons whole fennel seed

2 cups heavy cream

5 egg yolks

½ cup sugar

Pinch salt

½ teaspoon vanilla bean paste

Juice and finely grated zest
    of ½ orange

Caramel

4 to 6 tablespoons sugar

Serves 4 to 6

Catalonian Crème Brûlée

THE WORTHINGTON INN, WORTHINGTON
EXECUTIVE CHEF MICHAEL WATERS

The oldest portion of the Worthington Inn was built in 1831. Today it offers seasonal cuisine in a historical setting on the outskirts of Columbus. The menu offers a bit of the old and new, such as this compelling crème brûlée laced with orange zest and the toasty, sunny flavor of fennel seeds.

For the custard:
Preheat the oven to 300 degrees. Find a baking dish or roasting pan that will accommodate four to six crème brûlée dishes or ramekins without crowding.

Put the fennel seeds in a medium saucepan over medium heat and toast, stirring often, until aromatic, about 1 minute. Pour the cream into the pan and heat until a skin forms on the surface but it's not yet simmering. Remove from heat and set aside.

In a medium bowl, whisk the egg yolks with the sugar and salt to combine. Add the vanilla bean paste and orange juice. Slowly pour the infused cream into the bowl, stirring with the whisk all the while. Strain through a fine mesh strainer into another bowl, then stir in the orange zest.

Divide the mixture evenly between the dishes or ramekins. Add enough hot tap water to the larger pan to come halfway up the sides of the dishes. Bake until set, 35 to 40 minutes. Remove the baking pan from the oven. Let the custards cool in the water bath for 15 minutes, then remove them from the water and set on a wire rack to cool completely. Cover the custards with plastic wrap and chill in the refrigerator overnight.

(continued on page 132)

To caramelize and serve:

Remove the custards from the refrigerator. Pour about 1 tablespoon of the sugar on one of the custards and tip it around so the sugar is evenly distributed across the surface (dump any excess sugar onto the next custard). Repeat with remaining custards. With a culinary torch, caramelize the sugar to a nice, dark amber. Return the custards to the refrigerator for about 10 minutes to firm up the caramel, then serve.

Brownie layer

1 ¼ cups (2½ sticks) unsalted butter, cut into large cubes

2 cups (12 ounces) semisweet chocolate chips

4 ounces unsweetened chocolate, finely chopped

¾ cup all-purpose flour

2 teaspoons baking powder

½ teaspoon salt

5 large eggs

1 tablespoon vanilla extract

1¾ cups sugar

Hazelnut layer

⅔ cup chocolate-hazelnut spread (such as Nutella®)

1 tablespoon canola oil

Caramel layer

8 ounces soft caramels, unwrapped

6 tablespoons heavy cream

¾ cup roughly chopped toasted hazelnuts

Chocolate Hazelnut Layered Brownies

THE BISTRO AT GERVASI VINEYARD, CANTON
EXECUTIVE CHEF JERRY RISNER

The sophisticated flavor of hazelnuts elevates these brownies from a sweet nibble to an elegant stand-alone dessert. The baking and assembly take some time, so they are best made on a day when you plan to be in the kitchen for a while. They freeze beautifully and are best served in small squares, as they are insanely rich.

Preheat the oven to 350 degrees with a rack in the center of the oven. Line a 13 x 9–inch pan with baking parchment.

For the brownies:
Melt the butter in a large saucepan over medium heat, swirling the pan frequently. You want the butter to get hot, but not brown. Just when you hear the butter begin to sputter, remove the pan from the heat and drop in the semisweet and unsweetened chocolate. Stir once, let sit for 3 minutes, and then stir again with a rubber spatula until smooth.

Meanwhile, in a small bowl, whisk together the flour, baking powder, and salt. Set aside. In a large bowl, beat the eggs, vanilla, and sugar. Add the warm chocolate mixture and beat until well combined. Fold in the flour mixture with a rubber spatula until smooth (don't worry about overmixing). Pour half the batter into the prepared pan and spread evenly with an offset metal spatula. Cover the remaining batter and refrigerate. Bake until the batter is barely set, 10 to 12 minutes. Cool slightly, then freeze until cold, about 1 hour.

For the hazelnut layer:
Stir the chocolate-hazelnut spread and oil together in a small bowl. Spread over the cold brownie layer with a small offset metal spatula and return to the freezer until set, 30 to 60 minutes.

Garnish

2 ounces semisweet chocolate, finely chopped

¼ cup finely chopped toasted hazelnuts

Makes 3 to 4 dozen small brownies

For the caramel layer:
Meanwhile, heat the caramels and cream together in a microwave-safe bowl on 50 percent power in 1-minute increments, stirring after every minute, until smooth. (Alternatively, you may use a double boiler.) Spread the warm caramel over the chocolate–hazelnut layer and sprinkle with the chopped hazelnuts. Return to the freezer for 1 hour.

Again, preheat the oven to 350 degrees. Spread the remaining brownie batter on top and bake until the center is set but not too firm, 15 to 20 minutes. Cool completely on a wire rack and refrigerate until set.

Place a large cutting board over the pan, then invert. Peel off the parchment paper and discard. Set another large cutting board over the brownie bottom and invert again so the top faces up. Cut into 2-inch squares, and then cut each square into two triangles.

For the garnish:
To garnish, melt the semisweet chocolate and drizzle over the cut brownies. Sprinkle with the finely chopped hazelnuts and refrigerate until set.

The baked brownies will keep, refrigerated, for 1 week. Well wrapped, they may be frozen for up to 2 months.

Baking spray (optional)

1 tablespoon flaxseed meal

3 tablespoons water

1 cup whole wheat pastry flour

½ teaspoon baking powder

½ teaspoon baking soda

¼ teaspoon salt

⅔ cup organic sugar

⅔ cup non-hydrogenated vegan
 shortening, such as Spectrum

2 tablespoons molasses

½ teaspoon vanilla extract

1 cup rolled oats (not instant)

⅔ cup dried cranberries

⅔ cup chopped pecans

½ cup chocolate chips

¼ cup unsweetened shredded
 coconut

Makes 16 to 20 cookies

Everything Oatmeal Cookies

PATTYCAKE BAKERY, COLUMBUS

Worker-owned Pattycake Bakery offers delicious vegan treats for people of all dietary persuasions. This oatmeal chocolate chip cookie really does have a little bit of everything—except animal products. If you like, substitute different dried fruits and nuts for the cranberries and pecans.

Preheat the oven to 350 degrees with racks in the upper and lower thirds of the oven. Line two cookie sheets with parchment paper or grease them with a thin layer of oil or baking spray.

In a small bowl, combine the flaxseed meal and water. Set aside to thicken.

In a medium bowl, whisk together the flour, baking powder, baking soda, and salt. Set aside.

In the bowl of an electric mixer fitted with the paddle attachment, beat the sugar and shortening together until light and creamy. Add the molasses, vanilla, and flax mixture and beat until well combined. Add the flour mixture and beat until a sticky dough forms. Add the oats, cranberries, pecans, chocolate chips, and coconut with the mixer on low until just incorporated. (If the dough is too stiff to stir, add up to 1 tablespoon water.)

Scoop out the dough by rounded tablespoons onto the cookie sheets, twelve to a sheet. Flatten each dough ball slightly with your hand (the cookies will not spread much). Bake until the cookies are slightly brown at the edges, 12 to 14 minutes, rotating the pans top to bottom and front to back halfway through the baking time. Cool the cookies on the sheets for about 3 minutes, then remove to a wire rack with a thin metal spatula and let cool completely. Cookies will keep in a covered container for up to 4 days.

❧ **Note:** *If you want the cookies to be truly vegan, be mindful to read the ingredients of the chocolate chips you use. Many chocolate chips—even dark chocolate chips—contain milk fats. You can bake larger cookies using one scant ¼ cup of dough per cookie. The yield will be about a dozen cookies this way.*

Gingersnap and Jalapeño Bread Pudding (Capirotada)

MOMOCHO, CLEVELAND ❧ CHEF-OWNER ERIC WILLIAMS

People pack into Chef Williams' hip taqueria for his modern take on Mexican fare. Once the dinner plates are cleared, make way for this spicy dessert, not a run-of-the-mill bread pudding. The smooth custard is offset by the crunch of a turbinado sugar topping, while crushed gingersnaps and minced fresh jalapeño contribute a heat that's unexpected but not unwelcome.

4 large egg yolks

⅓ cup brown sugar

⅓ cup granulated sugar

1 cup milk

1 cup heavy cream

1 jalapeño, seeded, stemmed, and minced

1 teaspoon ground cinnamon

2 cups crumbled gingersnaps (about 22 cookies)

6 to 8 cups (about 8 ounces) cubed brioche

1 cup raisins

2 tablespoons turbinado sugar

Whipped cream, for serving (optional)

Serves 6 to 8

Preheat the oven to 350 degrees with a rack in the center of the oven. Grease an 8 x 8-inch baking dish.

In a large bowl, whisk together the egg yolks and brown and granulated sugar. Set aside.

Taste a little of the jalapeño. If it's quite spicy, you may want to only add part of it. In a medium saucepan, combine the milk, cream, jalapeño, and cinnamon. Slowly heat over medium-low heat, just until tiny wisps of steam start to rise. Remove from heat. Slowly whisk the warm cream mixture into the egg and sugar mixture.

Arrange the gingersnaps, brioche cubes, and raisins in the prepared baking dish and pour the egg mixture over the top. Let sit for 10 minutes.

Sprinkle the turbinado sugar on top and cover the pan with foil. Bake for 25 minutes. Rotate the pan, remove the foil, and bake for another 20 minutes, or until a toothpick inserted in the center of the pudding comes out clean. Set on a rack to cool somewhat.

Scoop or cut out portions and serve warm or chilled with whipped cream, if desired.

6 mini Nutter Butter cookies

1 ounce white crème de cacao,
    plus more for rimming the glass

1 ounce Irish cream liqueur

1 ounce Buckeye vodka

Chocolate syrup, for decoration

Makes 1 drink

Nutter Butter Buckeye Martini

BUCKEYE VODKA, DAYTON

Crafted in the Miami Valley, Buckeye vodka is known for its smooth-drinking character, one that plays well with other spirits. This martini may seem over the top on paper, but be careful—it's irresistible, and a first sip quickly leads to another.

Crush five of the cookies by muddling them in a glass or by putting them in a plastic bag and lightly bashing them with a rolling pin. Transfer the crushed cookies to a deep saucer. Pour a little crème de cacao in another saucer. To coat the rim of the glass, dip it in the crème de cacao and then into the crumbs.

Put equal parts crème de cacao, vodka, and Irish cream in a shaker with ice and shake. Drizzle the chocolate syrup along the sides of the martini glass to make a design. Strain the shaker into the glass. Garnish with a sprinkle of crushed cookies on top, or with a small cookie on the rim, and serve immediately.

(see photograph on page 125)

Old Fashion Cream Pie

DOUGHBOX BAKERY AT SAUDER VILLAGE, ARCHBOLD

This is a hometown favorite at the Doughbox Bakery at Sauder Village in Archbold. At 235 acres, Sauder Village is Ohio's largest living-history destination, offering visitors a taste of what life was like for Ohioans from the early 1800s to the 1920s. The on-site bakery makes hundreds of home-style cookies, pastries, and pies every day. Eggless custard pies like this were once standard fare, and they're worth resurrecting. The filling is smooth and dense and far more compelling than the simplicity of the ingredients suggests.

Crust

1 cup all-purpose flour

¼ teaspoon salt

½ teaspoon sugar

6 tablespoons unsalted butter, cold, cut into small pieces

2 to 4 tablespoons cold water

Filling

1 cup minus 2 tablespoons sugar

⅓ cup plus 1 tablespoon all-purpose flour

Pinch salt

2 cups heavy cream

1 teaspoon vanilla extract

Serves 6 to 8

For the crust:

In a large bowl, combine the flour, salt, and sugar. Add the cold butter and work with a pastry cutter or your fingertips until the mixture resembles coarse meal and no bits of butter larger than a pea remain. Toss in the water, 1 tablespoon at a time, until a shaggy but not dry dough forms (you may not need all of the water). Form into a disc, wrap in plastic wrap, and refrigerate for 30 minutes.

Roll the dough on a floured surface with a floured rolling pin to a 13-inch circle. Brush off any excess flour. Line a 9-inch pie plate with the dough. Trim the edges and crimp decoratively, if you like. Refrigerate the pie shell until firm, about 1 hour.

For the filling:

Preheat the oven to 350 degrees. In a large bowl, whisk together the sugar, flour, and salt until well combined. Fold in the cream and vanilla until smooth. Pour into the unbaked pie shell. Bake until the center is just a little jiggly, but a toothpick inserted in the pie comes out without runny liquid, about 1 hour. Cool completely on a wire rack before serving.

½ cup (1 stick) unsalted butter

1 cup sugar

1 cup self-rising flour (*see Note*)

¼ teaspoon cinnamon

¾ cup milk

1 (28-ounce) can peaches
   in light syrup

½ cup blueberries, fresh or frozen

Vanilla ice cream, for serving

Serves 6 to 8

Peach Blueberry Cobbler

STOCKPORT MILL INN & RESTAURANT ON THE DAM, STOCKPORT
OWNER DOTTIE SINGER

Perched right on the Muskingum River is a formidable mill, built in 1906. Milling operations there ceased in 1997, but today it's a distinctive bed and breakfast using hydroelectricity generated from turbines powered by the Muskingum. Balconies off the rooms offer a fascinating view of the spillway and the locks on the opposite side of the river. The restaurant offers delicious home-style food, such as this cakey fruit cobbler.

Preheat the oven to 350 degrees. Place the butter in the bottom of a 7 x 11–inch baking pan or a 10–inch deep–dish pie plate. Put in the oven until the butter is melted and sizzling hot.

In a large bowl, stir together the sugar, flour, and cinnamon. Add the milk and stir with a rubber spatula until a batter forms and no dry streaks remain. Pour the batter over the hot melted butter, reserving a couple tablespoons of batter. Do not stir.

Pour the peaches and their liquid over the batter. Do not stir. Sprinkle the blueberries down the center of the peaches. Do not stir. Drizzle the reserved batter on top of the fruit. Do not stir.

Bake until the filling bubbles briskly, the topping is golden brown in spots, and a toothpick inserted in the topping emerges free of gooey batter, 40 to 60 minutes. Serve warm or at room temperature with a scoop of vanilla ice cream.

  Note: *If you don't have self-rising flour, you may substitute 1 cup all-purpose flour mixed with 1½ teaspoons baking powder and ¼ teaspoon salt.*

2 cups sifted powdered sugar

¾ cup smooth peanut butter

4 tablespoons unsalted butter, melted

½ teaspoon vanilla extract

¼ teaspoon salt

12 ounces semisweet chocolate, finely chopped

½ teaspoon vegetable shortening

Makes about 2 dozen cookies

Peanut Butter Buckeyes

SARA BIR, THE SAUSAGETARIAN

The Ohio buckeye tree is the state tree of Ohio. While its shiny black nuts are lovely to gather up in the fall and admire, they are unpalatably tannic. For eating, you are much better off with this classic confection of dark chocolate and peanut butter. They're popular on holiday cookie platters throughout the region, and they blow a certain familiar peanut butter cup out of the water.

Line a baking sheet with parchment or waxed paper.

Combine the powdered sugar, peanut butter, butter, vanilla, and salt in a large mixing bowl and beat well with a wooden spoon (or knead together with your hands) until the dough is smooth and pliable but not sticky. Roll into 1-inch balls and transfer to the prepared baking sheet. Freeze until firm, 15 to 20 minutes.

Meanwhile, melt the chocolate and shortening in a small heat-safe bowl set over a saucepan of simmering water, stirring often until smooth. Remove from heat.

Insert a thin wooden skewer or toothpick into the center of a ball and dip about three-quarters of it into the melted chocolate, leaving a small circle of peanut butter exposed at the top. Transfer to the baking sheet. Remove the toothpick and repeat the dipping process with the remaining peanut butter balls and chocolate, reheating the chocolate briefly, if necessary.

For smoother centers, gently smooth over the skewer holes in the filling with your fingertip. Freeze or refrigerate the buckeyes until firm. They will keep in a covered container in a cool place for up to 1 week, and in the refrigerator for up to 2 weeks (but they'll be gone long before then).

Cherry-poached beets

30 petite beets (tops removed)
    or 6 large red beets

2 cups cherry juice

½ cup granulated sugar

1 rag or kitchen linen

Dough

1 cup whole wheat flour

½ cup almond flour

½ teaspoon salt

½ cup (1 stick) unsalted butter,
    room temperature

½ cup brown sugar

2 tablespoons milk

1 teaspoon vanilla extract

Powdered sugar, for dusting

Makes about 30 cookies

Petite Beet and Cherry Glazed Thumbprint Cookies

THE CULINARY VEGETABLE INSTITUTE, MILAN
CHEF LIAISON JAMIE SIMPSON

A dreamy combination of a retreat center, garden, and experimental-educational kitchen, the Culinary Vegetable Institute offers agri-culinary experiences for both visiting chefs and guests. CVI's Chef Jamie Simpson designs dishes around what's available in the garden that day. His trompe l'oeil cookies resemble peanut butter blossoms at first glance, but are really topped with tiny fruit-infused beets.

For the cherry-poached beets:
Place the beets in a medium saucepan and add just enough cherry juice to cover the surface of the beets. Poach at a very low, non-bubbling simmer until a wooden toothpick easily slides into the beets, about 30 minutes (if using full-size beets, it may take up to 2 hours of poaching).

Using a slotted spoon, lift the beets from the poaching liquid and set in a bowl until cool enough to handle. Add the sugar to the poaching liquid and cook over medium-low heat until reduced to a thick syrup. Set aside.

Meanwhile, using a clean rag or kitchen towel you don't mind staining, pull the skins off the beets, being careful to keep the root end intact. Discard the skins. (If using full-size beets, use a melon baller to make about thirty beet balls. They don't need to be perfect, as long as they are nicely domed on one side.)

Preheat the oven to 350 degrees with racks in the upper and lower thirds of the oven. Line two baking sheets with parchment or silicone baking mats.

For the dough:

In a medium bowl, whisk together the whole wheat flour, almond flour, and salt. In the bowl of an electric mixer fitted with the paddle attachment, beat the butter and brown sugar until light and fluffy. Add the flour mixture and combine on low speed. Add the milk and vanilla to make a soft, homogenous dough.

Scoop the dough by rounded teaspoons onto the lined baking sheets. Gently press your thumb into the center of the dough ball, forming a well just big enough for the beet ball to rest. Place the beet, root side up, into the well (if using melon–balled beets, place the domed side up).

Bake until the cookies are just beginning to turn golden brown at the edges, 10 to 15 minutes. Cool, then paint the beets with the cherry glaze using a pastry brush. Sift a dash of powdered sugar over the cookies and serve.

❧ **Note:** *You'll have leftover cherry syrup. Keep it in the refrigerator—it's delicious drizzled over plain yogurt.*

2 cups whole milk, divided

1 tablespoon plus 1 teaspoon cornstarch

3 tablespoons (1 ½ ounces) cream cheese, softened

½ teaspoon fine sea salt

1 ¼ cups heavy cream

⅔ cup sugar

2 tablespoons light corn syrup

1 cup fresh, unsalted popped corn (*see Note*)

Makes about 1 quart

Popped Corn Ice Cream

JENI'S SPLENDID ICE CREAMS, COLUMBUS
FOUNDER JENI BRITTON BAUER

From humble beginnings, Jeni Britton Bauer's inventive and flavor-forward ice creams quickly gained a rabid following. This recipe—which boasts incredibly buttery undertones despite having no butter at all—is great topped with caramel sauce and roasted peanuts, or all by itself on a cone.

To make and chill the ice cream base:
Mix about 2 tablespoons of the milk with the cornstarch in a small bowl to make a smooth slurry.

Whisk the cream cheese and salt in a medium bowl until smooth. Fill a large bowl with ice and water.

Combine the remaining milk and the cream, sugar, corn syrup, and popcorn in a 4-quart saucepan, bring to a rolling boil over medium-high heat, and boil for 4 minutes. Remove from heat and puree.

Strain the milk mixture through a sieve lined with a layer of cheesecloth, pressing on the popcorn to extract as much cream as possible. Return to the saucepan and whisk in the cornstarch slurry. Bring the mixture to a boil over medium–high heat and stir with a heat-safe spatula until slightly thickened, about 1 minute. Remove from heat.

Gradually whisk the hot milk mixture into the cream cheese until smooth. Pour the mixture into a 1-gallon zip-top freezer bag and submerge the sealed bag in the ice bath. Let stand, adding more ice as necessary, until cold, about 30 minutes.

To freeze:
Churn in an ice cream maker according to the manufacturer's directions until thick and creamy. Pack the ice cream into a storage container, press a sheet of parchment directly against the surface, and seal with an airtight lid. Freeze in the coldest part of your freezer until firm, at least 4 hours.

❧ **Note:** *If using pre-popped popcorn, decrease the amount of salt used.*

Pie

1 unbaked 9-inch pie crust

1 (16-ounce) box devil's food
cake mix

1 egg

½ cup (1 stick) unsalted butter,
melted

1 to 3 tablespoons water

¾ cup (4 ounces) thinly sliced
Snickers® candy bar pieces

To serve

Vanilla ice cream

Whipped cream

Caramel sauce

Chocolate syrup

Additional chopped Snickers® bar,
for garnish

Serves 8

Snickers® Candy Bar Cookie Pie

NUTCRACKER FAMILY RESTAURANT, PATASKALA
OWNER NANCY BUTCHER

*Nancy Butcher makes most of the pies at the diner she and her husband,
Steve, run. She created this recipe for General Mills' 2016 Neighborhood
to Nation Recipe Contest and took top honors in the dessert category. The
brownie-like pie quickly earned a regular spot in Nutcracker's expansive
pie selection. They go through at least two of these a day at the restaurant.*

For the pie:
Preheat the oven to 350 degrees with a rack in the center of the oven.
Line a 9-inch pie pan with the crust. Crimp the edges decoratively,
if you like.

Empty the cake mix into a large bowl. Add the egg, butter, and
1 tablespoon of water and work by hand until moistened. Add the
Snickers® slices and continue working until the mixture resembles
soft cookie dough. Add up to 2 more tablespoons water if the mixture seems dry. Press the mixture evenly into the crust. Bake until
the filling is puffed and a toothpick inserted in the center comes
out with gooey crumbs but no wet streaks, about 25 minutes (do
not overbake).

To serve:
Cool slightly. Serve warm or at room temperature, topped with
vanilla ice cream, whipped cream, caramel sauce, chocolate syrup,
and a few more chopped Snickers®. The pie will keep, covered, at
room temperature for 3 days.

⋈ ***Note:*** *Boxed cake mixes differ slightly. You may need to add more or less water,
depending on the brand you use. At the restaurant, Nancy divides one batch of
filling between two pie crusts to make two pies, serving 16. To do that, reduce
the baking time to 20 minutes.*

sources for specialty ingredients and other products

Air-dried red and green bell peppers: northbaytrading.com

Beef neck roast and fresh local meats from Na*Kyrsie Meats: nkmeats.com

Buckeye Vodka: find stores online at buckeyevodka.com

Canned truffle peelings: online at markeys.com

Cinnamon baking chips: online at kingarthurflour.com

Clear Jel: Ashery Country Store and other Amish bulk food stores, online at amazon.com

Diastatic malt powder: online at kingarthurflour.com

Dry-cured chorizo: online at spanishtable.com

Fresh Ohio-grown chestnuts: seasonally at route9cooperative.com

Fresh ramps: seasonally at Chesterhill Produce Auction, local farmers markets, or finer produce markets, or online from ledgerockfarms.com

Fresh and frozen pierogi: Ohio City Pasta or The Pierogi Place

Frozen pawpaw pulp and in-season fresh pawpaws: seasonally at local farmers markets and online at integrationacres.com

Goat milk Gouda: Turkeyfoot Creek Creamery and online at turkeyfootcreek.com

Goetta: goetta.com, or from Gramma Debbie's Kitchen at Cincinnati's Findlay Market

Great Lakes Brewing Company Dortmunder Gold beer: find stores online at greatlakesbrewing.com

Grumpy's Delicious Poppy Seed Dressing: online at grumpys.net

Guggisberg Baby Swiss cheese: major supermarkets and online at babyswiss.com

Herbs de Provence: North Market Spices and online at northmarketspices.com

Jarred whole roasted chestnuts: online at yummybazaar.com

Lake Erie perch: online at portclintonfish.com

Maumee Bay Brewing Co. Buckeye Beer: find stores at mbaybrew.com

Ohio maple syrup: online at ohiomaple.org, or try your local farmers market

Pastry flour: online at kingarthurflour.com

Scottish oats: finer supermarkets and online at bobsredmill.com

Shagbark spelt flour, cornmeal, and corn chips: find stores at shagbarkmill.com

Snowville Creamery yogurt and fresh dairy products: find stores at snowvillecreamery.com

Tony Packo's Pickles & Peppers: find stores or order online at tonypacko.com

Truffle butter: finer supermarkets

Walleye fillets: online at walleyedirect.com

Whole wheat pastry flour: finer supermarkets and online at kingarthurflour.com or bobsredmill.com

Wolf's Ridge Brewing Driftwood IPA: find stores at wolfsridgebrewing.com

Za'atar: North Market Spices and online at northmarketspices.com

contributors

9 Tables
11310 Jackson Drive
The Plains, OH 45780
(740) 707-4966
athensfinedining@gmail.com
athensfinedining.com

The 1861 Inn
300 North Riverside Drive
Batavia, OH 45103
(513) 735-2466
info@1861inn.com
1861inn.com

Amber Rose Restaurant
1400 Valley Street
Dayton, OH 45404
(937) 228-2511
amberrose@theamberrose.com
theamberrose.com

Arthur Morgan House
120 West Limestone Street
Yellow Springs, OH 45387
(937) 767-1761
innkeeper@arthurmorganhouse.com
arthurmorganhouse.com

Bar Dumaine
1061 Miamisburg-Centerville Road
Dayton, OH 45459
(937) 610-1061
host@bardumaine.com
bardumaine.com

The Barn Inn Bed and Breakfast
6838 County Road 203
Millersburg, OH 44654
(330) 674-7600
reservations@thebarninn.com
thebarninn.com

Beau's on the River
1989 Front Street
Cuyahoga Falls, OH 44221
(330) 920-7530
info@beausontheriver.com
beausontheriver.com

The Bistro at Gervasi Vineyard
1700 55th Street NE
Canton, OH 44712
(330) 497-1000
info@gervasivineyard.com
gervasivineyard.com

Brewfontaine
211 South Main Street
Bellefountaine, OH 43311
(937) 404-9128
cheers@brewfontaine.com
brewfontaine.com

Brick House on Main
Bed & Breakfast
529 East Main Street
Gnadenhutten, OH 44629
(330) 340-6451
brickhouseonmain@gmail.com
brickhouseonmain.com

Buckeye Vodka
827 South Patterson Boulevard
Dayton, OH 45402
buckeyevodka.com

The Buckley House
332 Front Street
Marietta, OH 45750
(740) 374-4400
info@bhrestaurant.com
bhrestaurant.com

Cameron's American Bistro
2185 West Dublin-Granville Road
Columbus, OH 43085
(614) 885-3663
cameronsamericanbistro.com

Canal Tavern of Zoar
8806 Towpath Road NE
Bolivar, OH 44612
(330) 874-4444
eat@canaltavernofzoar.com
canaltavernofzoar.com

Cap City Fine Diner
1299 Olentangy River Road
Columbus, OH 43212
(614) 291-3663)
info@cameronmitchell.com
capcityfinediner.com

Casa Nueva
6 West State Street
Athens, OH 45701
(740) 592-2016
food@casanueva.com
casanueva.com

Chalet in the Valley
5060 State Route 557
Millersburg, OH 44654
(330) 893-2550
info@babyswiss.com
chaletinthevalley.com

Clay Haus
123 West Main Street
Somerset, OH 43783
(740) 743-1326
clayhaus.com

The Cooking School at Jungle Jim's
International Market
5440 Dixie Highway
Fairfield, OH 45014
(513) 674-6059
cookingschool@junglejims.com
junglejims.com/cookingschool/

Crave
57 East Market Street
Akron, OH 44308
(330) 253-1234
eatdrinkcrave.com

Creekside Restaurant & Bar
8803 Brecksville Road
Brecksville, OH 44141
(440) 546-0555
info@creeksiderestaurant.com
creeksiderestaurant.com

Crosswinds Grille
at The Lakehouse Inn
5653 Lake Road East
Geneva, OH 44041
(440) 466-8668
info@crosswindsgrille.com
www.crosswindsgrille.com

The Culinary Vegetable Institute
12304 Mudbrook Road
Milan, OH 44846
(419) 499-7500
culinaryvegetableinstitute.com

Dante Restaurant
2247 Professor Avenue
Cleveland, OH 44113
(216) 274-1200
events@danteboccuzzi.com
dantetremont.com

Doughbox Bakery
at Sauder Village
22611 State Route 2
Archbold, OH 43502
(800) 590-9755
info@saudervillage.com
saudervillage.com

Easter House Bed & Breakfast
508 North Main Street
Ada, OH 45810
(419) 558-1071
admin@easterhouse.net
easterhouse.net

Ferrante Winery & Ristorante
5585 State Route 307
Geneva, OH 44041
(440) 466-8466
ferrantewinery.com

The Feve
30 South Main Street
Oberlin, OH 44074
(440) 774-1978
love@thefeve.com
thefeve.com

Fur Peace Ranch
39495 St. Clair Road
Pomeroy, OH 45769
(740) 992-6228
vanessa@furpeaceranch.com
furpeaceranch.com

Gramma Debbie's Kitchen
Findlay Market
1801 Race Street
Cincinnati, OH 45202
(513) 421-4726
gramma.debbie@zoomtown.com
findlaymarket.org/merchants/
gramma-debbies-kitchen

The Granary at Pine Tree Barn
4374 Shreve Road
Wooster, OH 44691
(330) 264-1014
info@pinetreebarn.com
pinetreebarn.com

Granville Inn
314 East Broadway
Granville, OH 43023
(740) 587-3333
info@granvilleinn.com
granvilleinn.com

Great Lakes Brewing Company
2516 Market Avenue
Cleveland, OH 44113
(216) 771-4404
GLBCinfo@greatlakesbrewing.com
greatlakesbrewing.com

Grumpy's
34 South Huron Street
Toledo, OH 43604
(419) 241-6728
grumpysdeli@gmail.com
grumpys.net

The House of Wines
4339 State Route 60
Marietta, OH 45750
(740) 373-0996
thehouseofwines@gmail.com
houseofwines.com

The Inn & Spa at Cedar Falls
21190 State Route 374
Logan, OH 43138
(740) 385-7489
info@innatcedarfalls.com
innatcedarfalls.com

The Inn at Brandywine Falls
8230 Brandywine Road
Northfield, OH 44067
(330) 467-1812
brandywinefallsinn@windstream.net
innatbrandywinefalls.com

The Inn at Dresden
209 Ames Drive
Dresden, OH 43821
(740) 754-1122
info@theinnatdresden.com
theinnatdresden.com

Jeni's Splendid Ice Creams
Multiple locations throughout Ohio
(614) 488-3224
contact@jenis.com
jenis.com

Malabar Farm Restaurant
3645 Pleasant Valley Road
Lucas, OH 44843
(419) 938-5205
info@malabarfarmrestaurant.com
malabarfarmrestaurant.com

Mancy's Steakhouse
953 Phillips Avenue
Toledo, OH 43612
(419) 476-4154
mancys.com

Maumee Bay Brewing Co.
27 Broadway Street
Toledo, OH 43604
(419) 243-1302
mbaybrew.com

Meadowlark Restaurant
5531 Far Hills Avenue
Dayton, OH 45429
(937) 434-4750
themeadowlark@bcglobal.net
meadowlarkrestaurant.com

Mecklenburg Gardens
302 East University Avenue
Cincinnati, OH 45219
(513) 221-5353
mecklenburggardens1865@gmail.com
mecklenburgs.com

Melanie Tienter
Monkey Business Photography
(740) 517-1646
mel.roby@yahoo.com
monkeybusinessphotos.com

Melt Bar & Grilled
Multiple locations in Ohio
meltbarandgrilled.com

Michael Anthony's at the Inn
21 West Main Street
Versailles, OH 45380
(937) 526-3020
michaelanthonysattheinn.com

Momocho
1835 Fulton Road
Cleveland, OH 44113
(216) 694-2122
eric@momocho.com
momocho.com

Moxie, the Restaurant
3355 Richmond Road
Beachwood, OH 44122
(216) 831-5599
info@moxietherestaurant.com
moxietherestaurant.com

Murphin Ridge Inn
750 Murphin Ridge Road
West Union, OH 45693
(937) 544-2263
murphin@bright.net
murphinridgeinn.com

Naslada Bistro
182 South Main Street
Bowling Green, OH 43402
(419) 373-6050
naslada@hotmail.com
nasladabistro.com

Nixtamalized
In and around Athens, Ohio
(See website for scheduled locations)
(740) 667-0409
info@nixtamalized.com
nixtamalized.com

North Market Spices, LTD
North Market
59 Spruce Street
Columbus, Ohio 43215
(614) 224-4107
ben@northmarketspices.com
northmarketspices.com

Nutcracker Family Restaurant
63 East Broad Street
Pataskala, OH 43062
(740) 964-0056
oldsweets@aol.com
nutcrackerpataskala.com

O Pie O
1527 Madison Road
Cincinnati, OH 45206
(513) 274-3238
lou@opieo.com
opieo.com

Ohio Pork Council
5930 Sharon Woods Boulevard #101
Columbus, OH 43229
(614) 882-5887
ohiopork.org

Ohio Sauerkraut Festival
10 B North Main Street
Waynesville, OH 45068
(513) 897-8855
barb@waynesvilleohio.com
sauerkrautfestival.com

Orchids at Palm Court
35 West 5th Street
Cincinnati, OH 45202
(513) 421-9100
orchidsatpalmcourt.com

Pattycake Bakery
3009 North High Street
Columbus, OH 43202
(614) 784-2253
info@pattycakebakery.com
pattycakebakery.com

Poco Piatti
3155 Chappel Drive
Perrysburg, OH 43551
(419) 931-0281
pocopiatti@gmail.com
pocopiatti.com

**The Refectory Restaurant
& Bistro**
1092 Bethel Road
Columbus, OH 43220
(614) 451-9774
refectory.com

Registry Bistro
144 North Superior Street
Toledo, OH 43604
(419) 725-0444
info@registrybistro.com
registrybistro.com

Rennick Meat Market
1104 Bridge Street
Ashtabula OH 44004
(440) 964-6328
info@rennickmeatmarket.com
rennickmeatmarket.com

Rip's Café
614 Youngstown-Poland Road
Struthers, OH 44471
(330) 755-0057

Rural Action
9030 Hocking Hills Drive
The Plains, OH 45780
(740) 677-4047
info@ruralaction.org
ruralaction.org

Salazar
1401 Republic Street
Cincinnati, OH 45202
(513) 621-7000
jose@salazarcincinnati.com
salazarcincinnati.com

The Sausagetarian
Sara Bir
(503) 764-9544
sausagetarian.com

**Schmidt's Restaurant
and Sausage Haus**
240 East Kossuth Street
Columbus, OH 43206
(614) 444-6808
info@schmidthospitality.com
schmidthaus.com

The Seasoned Farmhouse
3674 North High Street
Columbus, OH 43214
(614) 230-6281
tricia@theseasonedfarmhouse.com
theseasonedfarmhouse.com

Seasons Bistro and Grille
28 South Limestone Street
Springfield, OH 45502
(937) 521-1200
seasonsbistro@gmail.com
seasonsbistroandgrille.com

Shagbark Seed & Mill
88 Columbus Circle
Athens, OH 45701
(740) 590-2749
info@shagbarkmill.com
shagbarkmill.com

Sleepy Bee Café
3098 Madison Road
Cincinnati, OH 45209
(513) 533-2339
and
9514 Kenwood Road
Blue Ash, OH 45242
(513) 241-2339
queenbee@sleepybeecafe
sleepybeecafe.com

Snowville Creamery
32623 State Route 143
Pomeroy, OH 45769
(740) 698-2340
info@snowvillecreamery.com
snowvillecreamery.com

Sokolowski's University Inn
1201 University Road
Cleveland, OH 44113
(216) 771-9236
info@sokolowskis.com
sokolowskis.com

Stix Restaurant
110 East Sandusky Street
Findlay, OH 45840
(567) 525-3192
stixrestaurant@gmail.com
stixfindlay.com

**Stockport Mill Inn & Restaurant
on the Dam**
1995 Broadway Avenue
Stockport, OH 43787
(740) 559-2822
mill@stockportmill.com
stockportmill.com

Sycamore Farms Country Inn
3884 Wallace Road
Oxford, OH 45056
(972) 679-9898
sfcinn@gmail.com
sycamorefarmscountryinn.com

Tarragon at The Inn at Honey Run
6920 County Road 203
Millersburg, OH 44654
(330) 674-0011
info@innathoneyrun.com
innathoneyrun.com

Toledo Museum of Art Café
2445 Monroe Street
Toledo, OH 43620
(419) 255-8000
toledomuseum.org/visit/dining/

Tony Packo's
1902 Front Street
Toledo, OH 43605
(419) 691-6054
tonypacko.com

The Twisted Olive
5430 Massillon Road
North Canton, OH 44720
(330) 899-0550
info@thetwistedolive.com
thetwistedolive.com

The White Oak Inn
29683 Walhonding Road
Danville, OH 43014
(740) 599-6107
info@whiteoakinn.com
whiteoakinn.com

White Oaks Restaurant
777 Cahoon Road
Westlake, OH 44145
(440) 835-3090
woaks@att.net
white-oaks.com

Wolf's Ridge Brewing
215 North 4th Street
Columbus, OH 43215
(614) 429-3936
info@wolfsridgebrewing.com
wolfsridgebrewing.com

The Worthington Inn
649 High Street
Worthington, OH 43085
(614) 885-2600
kitchen@worthingtoninn.com
worthingtoninn.com

index